Between Husband & Wife

TALK TAPES BY DOUGLAS E. BRINLEY

After the Honeymoon . . . and Forever

Marital Relationships Seminar
(a four-tape set and booklet)

between
HUSBAND
&
WIFE

Gospel Perspectives
on Marital Intimacy

STEPHEN E. LAMB, M.D.
DOUGLAS E. BRINLEY, PH.D.

Covenant Communications, Inc.

Published by Covenant Communications, Inc.
American Fork, Utah

Printed in Canada
First Printing: March 2000

07 06 05 04 03 02 01 00   10 9 8 7 6 5 4 3 2

ISBN 1-57734-609-2

Contents

Introduction

Between Husband and Wife is about the sacred physical union of a man and woman in marriage. It is based on the premises that marriage, as ordained of God, is an essential doctrine of the Plan of Salvation (D&C 49:15–17; 131:1–4; 132:19–20, 24), and that a fulfilling sexual relationship profoundly enriches the marriage partnership. The greatest joy, the deepest satisfaction, and the most poignant impressions of the soul come to a man and woman in a covenant marriage by sharing emotional and physical intimacy.

"It is not good that the man should be alone," said our Father in Heaven of the unmarried Adam. "I will make him an help meet for him." And He did: a wonderful companion, Eve. Then the instruction, "Therefore shall a man leave his father and his mother, and shall cleave unto his wife: and they shall be one flesh" (Gen. 2:18, 24). Adam and Eve were forced to leave the ease of Eden to pioneer their fallen environment. Modern husbands and wives leave behind parents and siblings to strike out on their own. Both the command of Deity to be one and the magnetic power of attraction between the sexes ensure that the emotional and physical intimacy of marriage will more than compensate for the loss of association with parents and siblings.

Intimacy is designed to strengthen and validate marriage partners. A husband, in effect, tells his wife, "I love being married to you. I appreciate all you do to make my life enjoyable and wonderful.

Thank you for being my companion. I am honored to be your husband." A wife, in effect, responds, "I love being married to you, too. I enjoy our physical and emotional closeness and I'm grateful that we have each other." Such expressions of affection bring honor and enrichment to their union. The sharing of physical and emotional intimacy secures their friendship and companionship. Through such tender expressions, a husband and wife are united— whole and complete—and married life begins to fulfill the Creator's commandment to be one. Lehi's pronouncement that "Men [and women] are, that they might have joy" (2 Nephi 2:25) is confirmed.

When we speak of "emotional intimacy" in this book, we are referring to the process whereby married couples develop love and trust—a profound and personal sense of worth and acceptance. "Physical intimacy" becomes a sublime consummation of existing love and affection. The *Church Handbook of Instructions* offers this counsel: "Married couples also should understand that sexual relations within marriage are divinely approved not only for the purpose of procreation, but also as a means of expressing love and strengthening emotional and spiritual bonds between husband and wife," (158).

POTENTIAL DIFFICULTIES

Prior to marriage, most couples anticipate that the sexual dimension of their relationship will become one of the most enjoyable activities of their coming union. But, for a number of couples, this aspect of marriage turns out to be the most difficult part of their relationship. Instead of bringing joy and unity, physical intimacy is avoided—or at best tolerated. These couples may find physical intimacy to be a barren wasteland, or they may even turn it into a divisive battleground.

In truth, most couples struggle with sexual problems at some point in marriage. When these concerns are left unaddressed, intimacy, instead of enriching the marriage, can lead to heartache and distrust. "If you study the divorces as we have had to do in these past years," said President Spencer W. Kimball, "you will find there are . . . several reasons. *Generally sex is the first. They did not get along sexually*," (Kimball, *Teachings*, 312, emphasis added).

THE PURPOSE OF THIS BOOK

Our desire is to help married couples of all ages find greater satisfaction in their sexual union. Physical intimacy should enhance rather than detract from the partnership. God designed this relationship as a way for couples to soften hearts, bring a sense of oneness, appreciate their interdependence while acknowledging their dependence, initiate parenthood, and deal with the stresses and challenges of everyday living. Ideally, this adventure begins on the honeymoon and continues throughout life.

It is also our intention to help married partners avoid common sexual difficulties, whether these have their basis in physical limitations or psychological barriers. In both of these areas, there are bound to be occasional malfunctions and misunderstandings. Sometimes, the solution to a sexual problem is as simple as getting counsel or information from competent medical sources, since it is common to be uninformed or even misinformed regarding these subjects. Also, many individuals are unaware that routine procedures, medical advancements, or new medications may resolve problems we have come to accept as unalterable.

A couple can begin to provide solutions to sexual problems by openly discussing their feelings and physical responses. But this is not easy. Newly married couples are frequently uncomfortable talking about their anatomy and physiology and may be reluctant to share the deeply personal emotions associated with intimacy. However, over time, each couple needs to develop the ability to communicate clearly and honestly, listening to one another and providing gentle instruction as they discover the intricacies of their own sexual functioning. After all, sexual relations are a new event in their life together, and these intimate occasions require partners to provide information and feedback. The implicit blessings of intimacy require a degree of friendship and trust that allows the married couple to candidly communicate their thoughts and feelings, so that both partners can enjoy and find fulfillment in their sexual union.

A satisfying sexual relationship is not guaranteed in the marriage ceremony, nor are instructions included with the nuptial certificate. A couple must learn the art of intimacy together and discover in their own union the power to strengthen and ennoble their marriage.

Notwithstanding the superficial and spontaneous portrayal of sex in the movies and other media, sexual intimacy is something most couples will work at and refine throughout their married life. As they share in the beauties of sexual passion, wonderful things can happen that will lift the entire marriage to a higher level of caring, affection, and cooperation.

Truly fulfilling marital intimacy is based on mutual trust, loyalty, fidelity, continued courtship after marriage, unselfishness on the part of both partners, and nurturing the nonsexual areas of the companionship. In sexual relations, we give ourselves to our spouse in a profoundly intimate, trusting, and vulnerable way. If we are criticized, belittled, or put down in any way, the relationship can be permanently damaged. Hurtful behavior without repentance can dampen feelings of love and reduce the desire to be intimate again. A marriage needs ongoing maintenance and care, and the intimate side of marriage requires emotional sensitivity and careful attention to the feelings of both companions.

It is no secret that men and women view intimacy from different perspectives. In this book, we will discuss the desires and sexual responses of both sexes. We will also explore barriers to intimacy. Abnormal medical conditions and psychological problems often contribute to sexual dysfunction, and we will discuss what can be done in each case. We will examine the effects of aging and medication on the sexual response of older married couples. Impediments to sexual fulfillment in the early, middle, and later years of marriage will be reviewed. As we discuss these concerns, we will provide suggestions for responding to them. There is one chapter written expressly for husbands and another specifically for wives. Finally, we have offered our responses to twenty typical questions that come up in private interviews and discussions.

The authors, a physician and a family educator, have devoted much of their professional lives to helping couples overcome marital difficulties, including sexual dysfunction. We approach the subject from a gospel perspective, combining the inspired wisdom of Church leaders and counselors with medical insights and information. Although we do not intend this book to be a sex manual, we recognize a need to provide specific information on the physical processes of intimacy. However, the best source for help in your marriage must always be your spouse. Marital intimacy represents a profound eternal commitment, and partners must teach and learn from each other how to bring joy and honor to their union through the physical sharing of self.

Appropriate "sex education" can prevent many problems before they begin. Sexual inexperience does not have to equate to sexual ignorance or poor performance. Many years ago, President Hugh B. Brown said,

> Many marriages have been wrecked on the dangerous rocks of ignorant and debased sex behavior, both before and after marriage. Gross ignorance on the part of newlyweds on the subject of the proper place and functioning of sex results in much unhappiness and many broken homes. Thousands of young people come to the marriage altar almost illiterate insofar as this basic and fundamental function is concerned. . . . Some sound instruction in this area will help a man to realize the numberless, delicate differentiations and modifications in the life and reactions of the normal woman. (*You and Your Marriage,* 73–74.)

We have written this book because Church members are searching for answers to questions about sexual matters. However, due to a lack of gospel-based instruction, many are turning to secular and worldly writings and videos. This material often promotes the view that "anything goes" in marriage. We disagree strongly with such an approach. A husband or wife who introduces pornographic or blatantly sexual material into the marriage in an attempt to heighten the companion's interest in more frequent relations or more exotic sexual activity will almost invariably bring harm to the relationship, damaging the delicate threads of love that bind them. While it is true that a couple should determine for themselves the frequency and creativity of their intimacy, there are expressions of appetites and passions that exceed divine counsel.

We express appreciation to our own companions, Margie and Geri, for their love and inspiration in our lives. In addition, we express our gratitude to the married students who shared feelings and experiences and gave us permission to use their quotes. We have made minor editing changes for clarity and used fictional names where necessary.

We thank those who read drafts of the manuscript. Elizabeth Graul, M.D., Kent Gammette, M.D., Weatherford Clayton, M.D., Barbara Hurst, M.D., and Kaydon Lusty, CNM, offered useful insights and suggestions. Several colleagues in the College of Religious Education at BYU also reviewed this material and gave helpful comments. Finally, we wish to express our appreciation for the talented assistance of Tyler Moulton, our editor at Covenant, who helped shepherd this project along. Of course, we as the authors are solely responsible for the final content.

Stephen E. Lamb, M.D.   Douglas E. Brinley, Ph.D.

CHAPTER I

Better Marriage, Better Intimacy

Generally speaking, the quality of marital intimacy is related to the quality of the marriage relationship. Couples who struggle in their marriages tend to avoid physical contact, while happily married people find physical intimacy to be a natural expression of their feelings. Strengthening the love that exists between a couple will normally increase their desire for a healthy sexual relationship. Happily married couples find that physical touches—kisses, hugs, embraces, massages, sexual relations—provide enjoyment and therapy in the marriage.

The most effective way Latter-day Saints can improve their marriages, and thus their sexual intimacy in marriage, is to understand the true purpose and nature of marriage as outlined in Church doctrine. President Boyd K. Packer taught that "a knowledge of the principles and doctrines of the gospel will affect your behavior more than talking about behavior" (*Ensign*, May 1997:9). This chapter will briefly review the place and importance of marriage in the Plan of Salvation. When we understand these doctrines and principles, we will better understand the need to do our best as marriage partners. An important part of this effort includes the way we interact as husbands and wives in our physical relationship.

In 1995, President Gordon B. Hinckley introduced a proclamation concerning marriage and the family (*Ensign*, November

1995:105). In essence, this pronouncement outlined the principle that "marriage is ordained of God unto man," (D&C 49:15). This proclamation on the family reaffirmed the Church's position that marriage and family are important theological imperatives. Latter-day Saints are taught that marriage is the most important of all priesthood ordinances. Through temple marriage, a couple may be joined together not just for this life, but as partners for eternity.

Gospel doctrine reveals that in the premortal realm we were sons and daughters of God, brothers and sisters to each other. But for us to become husbands and fathers, wives and mothers, it was necessary for us to come to earth to obtain physical bodies. President Spencer W. Kimball explained: "It is the normal thing to marry. It was arranged by God in the beginning. . . . Every person should want to be married. There are some who might not be able to. But every person should want to be married because that is what God in heaven planned for us," (Kimball, *Teachings*, 291).

THE DOCTRINE OF MARRIAGE

Heavenly Father did not intend the husband-wife relationship to last only for this life. Adam and Eve were married by God before the Fall, and their actions in the garden did not negate their holy marriage. Although death does separate husband and wife briefly, it does not divorce them. After Adam and Eve died, they were reunited as companions in the spirit world. Elder Bruce R. McConkie explained:

> We have the power to perform a marriage, and we can do it so that the man and the woman become husband and wife here and now and—if they keep the covenant there and then made—they will remain husband and wife in the spirit world and will come up in glory and dominion with kingdoms and exaltation in the resurrection, being husband and wife and having eternal life. ("Celestial Marriage," 172.)

The resurrection restores our physical and spirit bodies to an immortal union, thus making it possible to continue as husband and wife eternally, for as resurrected beings, we cannot die again (Alma 11:45). If we have complied with the laws of God and faithfully observed our covenants during this life, we can be eligible for exaltation. Our temple sealing allows us and our posterity—adults sealed to their own spouses—to be part of an everlasting kingdom. If we live worthily, we will one day dwell together forever in the highest degree of the celestial glory (D&C 131:1–4).

Elder Robert D. Hales reminded us:

> An eternal bond doesn't just happen as a result of sealing covenants we make in the temple. How we conduct ourselves in this life will determine what we will be in all the eternities to come. To receive the blessings of the sealing that our Heavenly Father has given to us, *we have to keep the commandments and conduct ourselves in such a way that our families will want to live with us in the eternities.* The family relationships we have here on this earth are important, but they are much more important for their effect on our families for generations in mortality and throughout all eternity. (*Ensign,* November 1996:65, emphasis added.)

We will only be companions in the next life if we like each other here! Therefore, we must cultivate love and respect for each other while in this life, so that we want to be together forever.

THE HEAVENLY PATTERN

As mortals, we pattern our lives after a heavenly model. "Our theology begins with heavenly parents," said Elder Dallin H. Oaks, "and our highest aspiration is to be like them," (*Ensign,* May 1995:87). We are their offspring, and our gender began at the time of our spirit birth. The proclamation on the family states that each of us is "a beloved spirit son or daughter of heavenly parents," and "gender is an essential characteristic of individual premortal, mortal, and eternal identity and purpose." President Gordon B. Hinckley said, "I know of no doctrine which states that we made a choice when we came to earth as to whether we wished to be male or female. That choice was made by our Father in Heaven in his infinite wisdom," (*Ensign*, November 1983:83).

Our Heavenly Father apparently passed through a mortal experience similar to our own. "It is the first principle of the Gospel," the Prophet Joseph Smith taught, "to know for a certainty the character of God, and to know that we may converse with him as one man converses with another, and that he was once a man like us; yea, that God himself, the Father of us all, dwelt on an earth," (Smith, *Teachings*, 345–46).

Brigham Young taught that "God the Father was once a man on another planet" who "passed the ordeals we are now passing through . . . and knows all that we know regarding the toils, sufferings, life and death of this mortality," (*Discourses*, 22). Thus, our Heavenly Father, like our earthly parents, knows of our joys and sorrows and how to succor us.

Church leaders have explained that "all men and women are in the similitude of the universal Father and Mother, and are literally the sons and daughters of Deity. . . . Man, as a spirit, was begotten and born of heavenly parents, and reared to maturity in the eternal mansions of the Father, prior to coming upon the earth in a temporal body to undergo an experience in mortality," (Clark, *Messages*, 203, 205).

These statements help us understand that exaltation always involves a male and female, a husband and wife, and that no one achieves such promised glory in isolation. Righteous unmarried singles will yet have the opportunity to marry. "No blessing, including that of eternal marriage and an eternal family, will be denied to any worthy individual. While it may take somewhat longer," said President Howard W. Hunter, "perhaps even beyond this mortal life for some to achieve this blessing, it will not be denied," (*Ensign*, June 1989:76).

We are presently moving through the mortal phase of the Plan of Salvation, acquiring information and knowledge, priesthood power and ordinances, and experiences that will prepare us for exaltation. In our mortal state, we learn the proper use of agency. We do this here on earth, where we are unable to see or remember our heavenly home, and where the full consequences of our choices are not always immediate. Thus, our mortal life is a time to try, to evaluate, and to repent, before the Final Judgment consigns us to an eternal destiny. In mortality, we taste the bitter and the sweet side by side and make conscious choices that will determine our destiny. "Behold, here is the agency of man," the Lord told Joseph Smith, "and here is the condemnation of man; because that which was from the beginning is plainly manifest unto them, and they receive not the light. And every man whose spirit receiveth not the light is under condemnation," (D&C 93:31–32). In mortality we experience the joy of righteous obedience and the exquisitely painful consequences of sin.

Following the resurrection, the possibility of being eternal companions is open to us through the sealing power of the Melchizedek Priesthood, (D&C 132:19-20). If we were to remain alone, without a marital companion, our progress would be eternally limited (D&C 131:4).

ETERNAL MARRIAGE AND INCREASE

Exalted beings continue the family unit by begetting spirit children. President Marion G. Romney gave this simple explanation to an acquaintance:

> As to why we are here on earth, I reminded him of the self-evident fact that, as the offspring of God, we inherit the capability of reaching, in full maturity, the status of our heavenly parents just as we inherit from our mortal parents the capability to attain to their mortal status; and that since God has a body of flesh and bones, it was necessary and perfectly natural for us, his spirit offspring, to obtain such bodies in order that we might be like him; that coming to earth was the means provided for us to obtain these bodies. I further explained to him that this mortal probation provides us the opportunity to, while walking by faith, prove ourselves worthy to go on to perfection and exaltation in the likeness of our heavenly parents. (*Ensign,* May 1976:79.)

While mortal parents create mortal children, resurrected beings create spirit children. Elder Melvin J. Ballard explained the principle of eternal increase:

What do we mean by endless or eternal increase? We mean that through the righteousness and faithfulness of men and women who keep the commandments of God they will come forth with celestial bodies, fitted and prepared to enter into their great, high and eternal glory in the celestial kingdom of God, and unto them, through their preparation, there will come spirit children. I don't think that is very difficult to comprehend. The nature of the offspring is determined by the nature of the substance that flows in the veins of the being. When blood flows in the veins of the being, the offspring will be what blood produces, which is tangible flesh and bone; but when that which flows in the veins is spirit matter, a substance which is more refined and pure and glorious than blood, the offspring of such beings will be spirit children. (Ballard, "Three Degrees," 10.)

Joseph Smith also taught, "all will be raised by the power of God," in the resurrection, "having spirit in their bodies, and not blood," (*TPJS*, 199–200). Our sexual nature is not a temporary power limited to a brief period of mortality. If we receive exaltation, our resurrected bodies, like those of our heavenly parents, will be capable of procreation.

Satan's Damnation

Satan is damned forever from being a husband or a father. This is because spirits cannot reproduce or procreate. The Book of Mormon prophet Jacob explained that if there had been no Savior, then at death, we would become like Satan. "If the flesh should rise no more our spirits must become subject to that angel who fell from before the presence of the Eternal God, and became the devil, to rise no more. And our spirits must have become like unto him, and we become devils," (2 Nephi 9:8–9). If we were to remain spirits after death, we would lose our procreative powers, for spirits are unable to reproduce. Limited to a spirit body, we could not become parents ever again. And without the power of procreation, marriage would have no meaning, for in the Father's Plan, marriage and parenthood are linked together.

Satan lost the right to obtain a physical body because he chose not to sustain the Plan of Salvation. In addition to suffering the consequences, he also tried to remove agency from the Plan. He not only rebelled against the Father and the Son, but he sought to obtain their power (*see* Moses 4:1–4). He will never receive a physical body as we have. Consequently, he and his followers can never marry or become parents. "The adversary is jealous toward all who have the power to beget life," said Elder Boyd K. Packer. "He cannot beget life; he is impotent. He and those who followed him were cast out and forfeited the right to a mortal body," (*Ensign*, May 1992:66).

Jacob rejoiced in the "good news" of our deliverance: "O how great the goodness of our God, who prepareth a way for our escape from the grasp of this awful monster," (2 Nephi 9:9–10). The Savior's atonement and resurrection overcame the consequences of the Fall. "Is it any wonder, then," asked Elder Packer, "that in the Church marriage is so sacred and so important? Can you understand why your marriage, which releases these powers of creation for your use, should be the most carefully planned, the most solemnly considered step in your life? Ought we to consider it unusual that the Lord directed that temples be constructed for the purpose of performing marriage ceremonies?" (*Ensign*, July 1972:112).

THE CYCLE OF LIFE

Next to our discipleship, marriage is the most important of all commitments. "The most important step you have made or will make in your life is marriage," President Gordon B. Hinckley told a group of university graduates. "Its consequences are many, so important and so everlasting. No other decision will have such tremendous consequences for the future," (*Church News*, 1995:2). It is here in this life that we seek a companion, a sweetheart to whom we feel drawn and with whom we feel we can build an enduring relationship. Then, in marriage, we are commissioned to exercise our sexual powers to create physical bodies for the Father's spirit children. Perhaps in no more meaningful way do we approach the nobility and majesty of God and His work than through this endowment of procreation. God's work and His glory exist in the exaltation of His children, and we take part in that work as we nurture our children and raise them in righteousness (Moses 1:39).

Men learn from their wives how to serve effectively as husbands, while women learn from their husbands how to develop in their roles as wives. Parents learn how to be fathers and mothers from their children, and children are prepared for adulthood by their parents. Elder Packer said, "the ultimate purpose of all we teach is to unite parents and children in faith in the Lord Jesus Christ, that they are happy at home, sealed in an eternal marriage, linked to their generations, and assured of exaltation in the presence of our Heavenly Father," (*Ensign*, May 1995:8).

Temples

We organize and seal families together in temples. A priesthood sealer, representing Heavenly Father, unites a couple in an "order of the priesthood [meaning the new and everlasting covenant of marriage]," (D&C 131:2). Elder Bruce R. McConkie described his own experience of receiving these sacred ordinances with his new bride:

> I went to the temple, and I took my wife with me, and we kneeled at the altar. There on that occasion we entered, the two of us, into an 'order of the priesthood.' When we did it, we had sealed upon us, on a conditional basis, every blessing that God promised Father Abraham—the blessings of exaltation and eternal increase. The name of that order of priesthood, which is patriarchal in nature, because Abraham was a natural patriarch to his posterity, is the New and Everlasting Covenant of marriage. (McConkie, Research Seminar, 50.)

Elder Packer explained the need for both male and female in the temple setting:

> No man receives the fulness of the priesthood without a woman at his side. For no man, the Prophet [Joseph Smith] said, can obtain the fulness of the priesthood outside the temple of the Lord (D&C 131:1–4). And she is

there beside him in that sacred place. She shares in all that he receives. The man and the woman individually receive the ordinances encompassed in the endowment. But the man cannot ascend to the highest ordinances—the sealing ordinances—without her at his side. No man achieves the supernal exalting status of worthy fatherhood except as a gift from his wife. (*Ensign,* May 1998:73.)

APPLICATION

Courtship can help us to develop the kind of love that leads to marriage. When we marry in the temple, we enter the patriarchal order of marriage (D&C 131:1–4). We invite Heavenly Father's children to join our family unit and we devote ourselves to each other. Unfortunately, we make mistakes, but when we err, we apologize and do our best to make amends. Our potential for exaltation should be a motivating factor for us to do our best. "Except a man and his wife enter into an everlasting covenant and be married for eternity, while in this probation, by the power and authority of the Holy Priesthood," Joseph Smith taught, "they will cease to increase when they die; that is, they will not have any children after the resurrection," (*DHC* 5:391). A profound destiny awaits faithful couples who honor their covenants.

SUMMARY

The better our marriage, the better will be the quality of our intimacy. Emotional and physical contact between husband and wife enhances marital love, and the Lord has authorized these intimate expressions as one way to bring us closer to each other and to Him. Marriages are best strengthened when we incorporate the teachings and principles of the gospel of Jesus Christ into our lives and realize that His mission is essential to our having an eternal companionship. When we look longingly towards eternity, we desire to bring our agency into harmony with eternal principles. Marital intimacy is a temporary opportunity that will be made permanent if we obey gospel principles, honor priesthood ordinances, and keep our covenants with God, building a relationship together that is worthy of exaltation.

CHAPTER 2

Sexual Intimacy in Marriage

Sexual intimacy in marriage plays many important roles. President Ezra Taft Benson stated: "Sex was created and established by our Heavenly Father for sacred, holy, and high purposes," (Benson, *Teachings*, 409). Unfortunately, many married individuals are uncertain about sex, and for some, questions remain long into their marriages. They wonder: "Is it normal to have sexual urges?" "Is it truly acceptable to God to have sexual relations with my spouse?" "Is it appropriate to touch my spouse in private areas after we are married?" "Is nudity in front of my companion really all right?" One young man wrote, "My wife and I awoke on our first honeymoon morning, looked at each other and said, 'Is what we did last night really okay, or are we in trouble?'"

Statements such as this indicate that some young people are confused about sex. They understand the importance of temple marriage and the need to remain chaste in preparation for marriage, so they steel themselves against Satan's temptations. Much to their credit, they pursue personal purity in spite of their natural curiosity, considerable pressure from peers, and a well-orchestrated effort "in the hearts of conspiring men in the last days," (D&C 89:4) to lead them away from virtue and truth. Simply, they learn to say "no" to sex because they know it is wrong for them, just as they learn to say "no" to drugs, alcohol, and other dangerous things.

It is not surprising, therefore, that some youth approach marriage with uncertainty and internal conflict about sexual matters. They wonder about saying "yes" to their spouse after saying "no" for so long. Perhaps in our attempts to encourage young people to be chaste, we sometimes send an unbalanced message. Have we failed to convey the peace of mind that comes through self-control before marriage and the exultant joy of proper sexual intimacy afterward? Have we not fully explained that God Himself instructed His children to participate in sexual relations as an important aspect of the marriage covenant?

LDS couples, young and old, need to know that sexual relations within marriage are not merely acceptable to the Lord; they are encouraged and ordained by Him. "Husband and wife . . . are authorized, in fact they are commanded to have proper sex," President Kimball said, "when they are properly married for time and eternity," (Kimball, *Teachings,* 312). A knowledge of the divinely ordained purposes of sexual intimacy can help individuals approach marriage with less trepidation, allowing them to enjoy the marital union more freely and without inappropriate guilt or concern.

Latter-day Church leaders have taught that there are at least four purposes for sexual intimacy in marriage (these are not in any order):

    1. To provide a profound expression of love

    2. To bring emotional and physical closeness

    3. To fulfill God's commandment to have children

    4. To experience pleasure and joy

Let's look at each of these more closely.

TO PROVIDE A PROFOUND EXPRESSION OF LOVE

The first purpose of sexual intimacy is to provide an expression of love. It is perhaps the most sublime way for a married couple to say, "I love you." Elder Parley P. Pratt expressed his thoughts on the love to be found in marriage:

> Our natural affections are planted in us by the Spirit of God, for a wise purpose; and they are the very main-springs of life and happiness—they are the cement of all virtuous and heavenly society—they are the essence of charity, or

love. . . . There is not a more pure and holy principle in existence than the affection which glows in the bosom of a virtuous man for his companion. (Robinson, 52.)

President Kimball, who often spoke and wrote on sensitive topics related to marriage, said:

> Sex is for procreation and expression of love. It is the destiny of men and women to join together to make eternal family units. In the context of lawful marriage, the intimacy of sexual relations is right and divinely approved. There is nothing unholy or degrading about sexuality in itself, for by that means men and women join in a process of creation and in an expression of love. (Kimball, *Teachings,* 311.)

Unfortunately, Satan has intentionally sought to blur the line between sex and love. He would lead people to believe that sex is love and that love can only be expressed through sexual relations. This is a devilish distortion that many people have accepted, much to their eventual disappointment. The truth is that marital love is more profound than sex, although sex is a powerful way for a couple to express their devotion to each other. Physical intimacy is an important part of marriage, but it is only one part. Indeed, any attempt to build a lasting marriage on this element alone will be unsuccessful.

To Bring Emotional and Physical Closeness

The second purpose of marital intimacy is to foster emotional and physical closeness between spouses. When a man and woman come together as married partners, they bring with them a lifetime of experience and expectations. Soon after the wedding ceremony, they discover that their spouse doesn't share all their cherished views, a fact that was not so apparent during the heady days of dating and courtship. They learn that they have differences that stem from their distinct personalities or cultural and family backgrounds. As a result, husbands and wives often have different approaches to handling problems, making decisions, resolving conflicts, raising children, managing finances, and dealing with other activities. These differences can challenge the fragile stability of their newly formed union.

The Lord designed sexual intimacy as one way for marriage partners to bring emotional closeness back into a relationship that may often become frayed in the tussle of day-to-day married life. Through physical closeness, spirits are buoyed and feelings are soothed. Partners are reassured and commitment is rejuvenated. Through the selfless giving of themselves, a couple learns how dependent they are upon each other for emotional and spiritual sustenance. Elder Packer expressed this sentiment:

> It is interesting to know how man is put together— how incomplete he is. His whole physical and emotional and for that matter, spiritual nature, is formed in such a way that it depends upon a source of encouragement and power that is found in a woman. When man has found his wife and companion, he has in a sense found the other half of himself. He will return to her again and again for that regeneration that exalts his manhood and strengthens him for the testing that life will give him. (Packer, *Tribune.*)

Certainly, this is also true for the woman. When a woman finds her eternal companion, she has found the other half of herself as well.

President Packer used the word "regeneration" in the above citation when talking about marital intimacy. The sexual union is one way marriage commitments can be renewed. Elder Jeffrey R. Holland referred to this as the sacramental nature of marital intimacy (*Ensign*, November 1998:75). While serving as president of Brigham Young University, he said:

> Sexual intimacy is not only a symbolic union between a man and a woman—the uniting of their very souls—but it is also symbolic of a union between mortals and Deity, between otherwise ordinary and fallible humans uniting for a rare and special moment with God himself and all the powers by which he gives life in this wide universe of ours.
>
> In this latter sense, human intimacy is a sacrament, a very special kind of symbol. Sexual union is also, in its own

profound way, a very real sacrament of the highest order, a union not only of a man and a woman but very much the union of that man and woman with God. Indeed, if our definition of sacrament is that act of claiming and sharing and exercising God's own inestimable power, then I know of virtually no other divine privilege so routinely given to us all—women or men, ordained or unordained, Latter-day Saint or nonLatter-day Saint—than the miraculous and majestic power of transmitting life, the unspeakable, unfathomable, unbroken power of procreation. (Holland, *BYU*, 82–83.)

The Lord provided marital intimacy as a way for couples who are occasionally pulled apart by the world to come together again and be reminded of their commitments to each other. It is an act of regeneration and healing whereby each spouse is validated anew. If offenses have been committed, it is the final gesture of a repentant heart. Through this sacrament, the husband and wife, in effect, say, "I'm sorry for my part in what happened. I'm glad it's behind us. I will do better. I'm grateful for you. I want you to know I always want to be with you. Thank you for being my dearest friend."

To Fulfill God's Commandments to Have Children

The third purpose of sexual intimacy in marriage is to provide the means whereby Heavenly Father's spirit children can enter their mortal estate. Adam and Eve received this injunction from a loving Father. "And God blessed them, and God said unto them, Be fruitful, and multiply, and replenish the earth," (Genesis 1:28). In the proclamation on the family, the importance of this commandment was re-emphasized by the First Presidency and Council of the Twelve:

The first commandment that God gave to Adam and Eve pertained to their potential for parenthood as husband and wife. We declare that God's commandment for His children to multiply and replenish the earth remains in force. We further declare that God has commanded that the sacred powers of procreation are to be employed only between man and woman, lawfully wedded as husband and wife. (*Ensign,* November 1995:102.)

Church leaders have emphasized that divinely given sexual urges help God fulfill His purposes, and hence are divinely approved. These feelings are intended to remind us of our responsibility to become parents for God's spirit children. They attract men and women to each other and give them a desire to marry and fulfill their divine natures, rather than remain single. What a sacred privilege! No wonder God holds individuals accountable for their procreative stewardship.

The power of procreation is a gift that enables men and women to act as co-creators with God in providing physical bodies for His spirit children. Because of its great importance in the eternal plan, President Kimball taught the importance of not delaying or inappropriately limiting the opportunity of parenthood (Kimball, *Teachings*, 324). Unless special circumstances exist (e.g., genetic problems, health considerations) every couple should anxiously desire to become parents. However, this responsibility requires considerable thought and planning, a consideration of the emotional and physical welfare of the mother, and the ability of the husband to function as a father and provider. Each couple must make this decision in a spirit of humility and prayer, seeking the Lord's blessing and guidance in fulfilling their responsibility (Benson, *Teachings*, 513).

The questions of how many children to have and how to space them require personal decisions each couple must make through the use of individual agency. Elder Dallin H. Oaks counseled:

> How many children should a couple have? All they can care for! Of course, to care for children means more than simply giving them life. Children must be loved, nurtured, taught, fed, clothed, housed, and well started in their capacities to be good parents themselves. Exercising faith in God's promises to bless them when they are keeping his commandments, many LDS parents have large families. Others seek but are not blessed with children or with the number of children they desire. In a matter as intimate as this, we should not judge one another. (*Ensign*, November 1993:75.)

The words of President Hinckley are also instructive:

> I like to think . . . of the meaning and sanctity of
> life, of the purpose of this estate in our eternal journey, of
> the need for the experiences of mortal life under the great
> plan of God our Father, of the joy that is to be found only
> where there are children in the home, of the blessings that
> come of good posterity. When I think of these values and
> see them taught and observed, then I am willing to leave
> the question of numbers to the man and the woman and
> the Lord. (Hinckley, *BYU,* 11.)

With conception and pregnancy, couples join hands with God in
the amazing and incomprehensible process of giving life. Who can
fathom the biological and spiritual implications of procreation? Being
partners with God as a co-creator is associated with spiritual dimensions which, for some, enhances the sexual experience. "When I was
younger, on the occasions when we were trying to get pregnant, the
sexual experience was accompanied by the most sublime joy," said
one woman who is now beyond childbearing years. "It was wonderful
to think that a new life might be conceived through that sacred act. I
miss those days." Because of the effects of age, this woman has
temporarily lost her ability to create life in partnership with God.
However, she finds great joy in anticipating the possibility of childbirth and parenting throughout eternity.

When children are born, parents are created. Parenthood brings
new opportunities for growth and happiness in what is perhaps the
toughest undertaking in life. But parenthood is also associated with
great blessings. It seems that as men and women learn to be good
parents, they are blessed with growing experiences. They often
develop traits that cannot be gained in any other way. Women learn
what it means to have sorrow and conception multiplied. Men learn
what it means to eat bread by the sweat of their face all the days of
their lives (Genesis 3:16, 17, 19). In addition, they experience the joy
that comes from interacting with their children throughout life.

Fortunately, we are given special gifts to help us fulfill our responsibilities as parents. Our premortal spiritual capacities, our genetic

endowments, and our individual personalities suit us to our roles as mothers and fathers. Then, through righteous parenting, we begin to acquire some of the characteristics of our Heavenly Parents and become more like them.

TO EXPERIENCE PLEASURE AND JOY

Finally, sexual intimacy is intended to provide joy. Heavenly Father knew that marriage would require effort, but that it could not be all work and no play. Marital intimacy is a way in which couples find diversion together. It is a form of therapy. It is a nice distraction from paying the mortgage, earning a living, keeping the cars running, paying the bills, and dealing with the children.

Sexual relations are designed to lift a marriage relationship from the profane and mundane to a higher plane. The pleasure of physical intimacy should motivate a couple to treat each other with increasing kindness and consideration. Indeed, the feelings of love and caring generated through sexual union normally carry over into their nonsexual relationship as well (Robinson, 254). President John Taylor spoke of the power of marital intimacy to provide "life, happiness, and exaltation" to marriage. He said:

> Well, he [God] has planted, in accordance with this, a natural desire in woman towards man, and in man towards woman and a feeling of affection, regard, and sympathy exists between the sexes. We bring it into the world with us, but that, like everything else, has to be sanctified. An unlawful gratification of these feelings and sympathies is wrong in the sight of God, and leads down to death, while a proper exercise of our functions leads to life, happiness, and exaltation in this world and the world to come. (*Gospel Kingdom,* 61.)

President Joseph F. Smith stated that sexual union blesses and sanctifies those who participate: "Sexual union is lawful in wedlock, and if participated in with right intent is honorable and sanctifying. But without the bonds of marriage, sexual indulgence is a debasing sin, abominable in the sight of Deity," (*Gospel Doctrine,* 309).

Church leaders have affirmed that sexual intimacy in marriage is intended to enrich marriage. "Husbands and wives do have physical and emotional needs that are fulfilled through sexual union. . . . Becoming as one flesh can be one of life's richest and most rewarding experiences," (*A Parent's Guide*, 49).

Lehi taught his son Jacob, "Men are that they might have joy," (2 Nephi 2:25). The pursuit and attainment of joy is one of the primary purposes of life. Joy is attained when our lives are in harmony with the will of God and his purposes, and when we are in harmony with each other. Sexual intimacy in marriage is one way in which joy is shared. President Taylor underscored this fact:

> What is more amiable and pleasant than those pure, innocent, endearing affections which God has placed in the hearts of the man and woman, who are united together in lawful matrimony? With a love and confidence pure as the love of God, . . . they live together in the fear of God, enjoying nature's gifts uncorrupted and undefiled as the driven snow, or the crystal stream. (*Government* Chapter 5.)

The enjoyments of life rightfully include the sensations and emotional feelings that are generated by being physically close to each other. It is relaxing and pleasurable for couples to massage, stimulate, and arouse each other. These passions, when kept with the bounds of propriety, become sanctifying and enriching to each spouse and to the marriage.

Men and women were anatomically created in such a way that feelings of acute pleasure are produced during sexual activity. *A Parent's Guide*, published by the Church, emphasizes this idea:

> We would do well to ever remind ourselves of our first mortal parents. Instructing them, Heavenly Father commanded them to give attention to the whole range of their powers and passions. They were to subdue the earth, create and nurture posterity, become one flesh physically, cleave unto each other socially and emotionally, and learn to serve the purposes of God. They, as we, were endowed

with bodies, parts, and passions after the image of the Creator. This implies that as we, the children of God, develop virtuously within marriage we will discover ever more profound enjoyments of all his creations, including our own emotions, bodies, and spiritual capacities. (*A Parent's Guide*, 49.)

SUMMARY

Sexual union in marriage is intended to be enriching and exciting, pleasurable and joyful. One young newlywed said, "I never dreamed before marriage that it could be the source of spiritual binding so strong that it has caused us both to cry with tears of great joy." This kind of joy comes when we understand why God has given us the gift of marital intimacy and when we use that gift wisely. It comes when we are "one" in the highest sense of the word—one in purpose, desire, aspirations, and deeds. It occurs when we are faithful in our dedication to the marriage and place our spouse's sexual satisfaction ahead of our own. When this happens, we more fully understand why Elder Pratt called it "the very main-springs of life and happiness," (Robinson, 52).

CHAPTER 3

Enjoyable Marital Intimacy

Three simple, yet essential elements are necessary for married couples to enjoy their sexual union: a healthy marriage, a basic understanding of male and female sexual responses, and an environment of mutual trust that is free from physical, emotional, and spiritual barriers. Each of these elements will be discussed briefly in this chapter.

A STRONG, HEALTHY MARRIAGE

Obviously, every couple needs a strong and healthy marriage for intimacy to be rewarding. We keep stressing this point because it escapes too many people who focus on the sexual component of marriage without attempting to nurture the total relationship. A healthy marriage implies that a husband and wife are genuinely good friends and companions. They enjoy talking, sharing, touching, laughing together, and they look forward to being together, even after short periods of separation. They are inspired by one another and purposely lift each other in positive ways. Most of all, they just like each other. President Gordon B. Hinckley expressed this thought: "I am satisfied that a happy marriage is not so much a matter of romance as it is an anxious concern for the comfort and well-being of one's companion," (*Ensign*, May 1991:73). When we care about our spouse to the extent that his or her concerns become ours, and we care about our spouse's welfare as much as we do our own, we begin to learn what true love really means.

No marriage is perfect, of course. J. Golden Kimball reportedly said: "I have often wondered what would happen if a perfect man married a perfect woman. I'll bet he would shoot her inside of a week if she didn't poison him first," (Richards, *Kimball,* 100). Our task is not to re-make our spouse into our own image, as if we came from the "true" family while our spouse came from an inferior one. We all have days when we are less than spectacular; we disappoint ourselves and our spouse. We may even disagree on a number of issues. But we do our best to treat each other's ideas with respect, kindness, and deference. When we err, we seek forgiveness. As we exercise compassion and charity, each aspect of our relationship as husband and wife will grow.

Fulfilling marital intimacy has far more to do with the quality of the relationship than with physical technique. When both individuals do their best in their respective areas of responsibility in the home, and when both are mature enough to help each other in the common tasks of child-rearing, money management, housekeeping chores, and child-discipline, family life tends to run much smoother. For example, a wife's sexual interest (often to the amazement of her husband) is determined more by how he treats the children and takes responsibility at home than his brand of aftershave. If he initiates and helps prepare for family activities—prayer, scripture study, family home evening, family councils, church attendance—his wife will be more likely to appreciate his romantic overtures. Kevin Leman's book provides both a title and sermon: *Sex Begins in the Kitchen.* When we function well in the nonsexual areas of marriage, we will likely find greater enjoyment in our intimate times together.

HUMAN SEXUAL RESPONSES

The second requirement of good marital sex is to know some basic facts about male and female biology. Most of us are pretty illiterate before marriage when it comes to the sexual functioning of the opposite gender, and even of our own bodily responses. It is helpful for both husbands and wives to have at least a rudimentary understanding of human anatomy and physiology and a basic knowledge of what happens before, during, and after sexual intercourse. Although most couples, in time, figure these things out on their own, the marriage can benefit greatly from some simple education in advance. Whether that advice or counsel comes from a parent, a bishop, a trusted friend, or from competent literature, it is helpful to have some factual information before marriage.

An Environment of Trust

Third, an enriching sex life thrives in a marriage where there is an absence of physical, psychological, and spiritual barriers that negatively affect function and response and hinder pleasure and enjoyment. Physical barriers include health conditions such as endometriosis and urethritis, both of which can cause painful intercourse. Psychological barriers, as we will describe them, include emotional, social, and spiritual problems that deter or prevent sexual fulfillment. A history of mental or physical abuse may complicate marital intimacy for one or both partners. Significant family problems in the home can also become a worrisome distraction. When a teenager is uncooperative and mom and dad do not approach the situation as a team, or when finances are a pressing issue, the quality of intimacy will be affected. Selfishness, adultery, and personal depression can all exact heavy tolls on marital relationships. In other words, a fulfilling and therapeutic sexual life is promoted by good physical health, a clear conscience, and the gradual healing of former hurts.

The refuge of a righteous covenantal marriage provides an atmosphere of safety, a secure haven wherein two souls can remove the emotional walls they may have constructed around themselves and fully receive the love felt and expressed by a spouse. In sexual activities, we give ourselves to each other and assume a mutual trust in doing so. Within the appropriate boundaries established by the covenants we have made, sexual union offers a unique opportunity to share our very soul with our eternal companion. Should our vulnerability be violated, the walls return and we become hesitant to accept or express our love in such an honest and intimate way again.

In marriage, we pledge our fidelity and lay the foundation of a commitment that can progress through the eternities. Happily married couples find that healthy physical and emotional intimacy protects against the temptations of the adversary, which could otherwise lure one away from the Spirit and the sacred covenants of the gospel. When marriage ties are strong, we more easily resist any diversion from eternal goals. President Gordon B. Hinckley expressed his concern on this matter to women in the workplace. "You women who are single, and some of you who are married . . . may I give you a word of caution. You work alongside men. More and more, there are invitations to go to lunch, ostensibly to talk about business. You travel together. You stay in the same hotel. You work together. Perhaps you cannot avoid some of this, but you can avoid getting into compromising situations. Do your job, but keep your distance," (*Ensign*, November 1998:99).

President Ezra Taft Benson counseled husbands,

> If you are married, avoid flirtations of any kind. Sometimes we hear of a married man going to lunch with his secretary or other women in the office. Men and women who are married sometimes flirt with and tease members of the opposite sex. So-called harmless meetings are arranged or inordinate amounts of time are spent together. In all of these cases, people rationalize by saying that these are natural expressions of friendship. But what may appear to be harmless teasing or simply having a little fun with someone of the opposite sex can easily lead to more serious involvement and eventual infidelity.
>
> If you are married, avoid being alone with members of the opposite sex whenever possible. Many of the tragedies of immorality begin when a man and woman are alone in the office or at church or driving in a car. At first there may be no intent or even thought of sin. But the circumstances provide a fertile seedbed for temptation. One thing leads to another, and very quickly tragedy may result. It is so much easier to avoid such circumstances from the start so that temptation gets no chance for nourishment. (Benson, *BYU,* 52.)

Couples who like each other generally find their determination to keep personal covenants is strengthened, and they can avoid sexual transgressions, which are so detrimental to marriage relations. Adultery is devastating to a covenantal relationship. Such a liaison represents a complete betrayal of everything holy about marriage. An individual who has accepted the holy promises of marriage and who then seeks the intimate company of another becomes a traitor to covenants, common sense, and spousal loyalty, all of which are integral components of the marriage commitment. Breaking the heart of a companion through infidelity is a sin of major proportions. Not only is repentance long and difficult, but when the fragile thread of trust between companions has been broken, it is challenging, and sometimes impossible, to restore the relationship to its former state. As Elder Boyd K. Packer taught,

> To willfully destroy a marriage, either your own or that of another couple, is to offend our God. Such a thing will not be lightly considered in the judgments of the Almighty and in the eternal scheme of things will not easily be forgiven.
>
> Do not threaten nor break up a marriage. Do not translate some disenchantment with your own marriage partner or an attraction for someone else into justification for any conduct that would destroy a marriage. (*Ensign,* May 1981:14.)

SUMMARY

As couples, we set the stage for fulfilling marital intimacy through our respect and appreciation for each other. Sexual relations were intended by Deity to enrich marriage. As we learn more about our individual sexual responses and avoid physical, psychological, or spiritual barriers, our enjoyment of emotional and physical intimacy is enhanced.

CHAPTER 4

The Human Sexual Response

A basic knowledge of human biology can aid every married couple in their efforts to have a meaningful intimate life together. Even a rudimentary understanding of physiology and anatomy can help them avoid problems and enhance sexual fulfillment. Knowledge decreases fear of the sexual experience, increases awareness of personal and spousal responses, and improves one's ability to be a better partner in this intimate facet of marriage.

Prior to about 1966, the information in medical and social literature regarding the human sexual response was neither completely accurate nor commonly available. Individuals who were preparing for marriage or married couples having sexual problems could not easily obtain reliable information to better understand their situation. They were left to rely on family and friends for advice.

Today, sexual matters are the subject of rigorous investigation by researchers from a variety of disciplines. An abundance of data on human sexuality is now accessible to the average reader. Although some questions remain unanswered, the human sexual response is now fairly well understood. We now know, for example, about the phases of the sexual response and the specific physiologic and anatomic changes that occur in normal and abnormal situations.

Although a knowledge of sexual matters can be of great value, the current avalanche of material has a potential downside. It can titillate and lead to sexual experimentation outside the bounds of marriage. It can also create unrealistic expectations and performance pressures for those who are married. Hence, the need for a balanced perspective within a gospel framework, one where an understanding of biology is accompanied by direction from scriptures and inspired leaders, and where sexual desires are kept within the bounds the Lord has set.

This chapter presents a straightforward discussion of the anatomy and physiology of the sexual response. It is intended as a foundation for a more complete understanding of marital intimacy. However, only a general description is given here. The details are left for each couple to fill in for themselves. Individuals should not be distressed if they find they don't exactly match the sexual responses described in popular writings or medical textbooks, especially since some sources contain sensationalized descriptions. If a couple's sexual experience is emotionally and physically enriching and a source of pleasure and renewal, then sexual relations are in harmony with their God-given purpose.

The Phases of the Human Sexual Response

The human sexual response is a multistage process that follows certain basic sequences. Historically, several models have been used to describe this phenomenon. The most simple model was proposed in 1979 by Helen Singer Kaplan (*see* Kaplan, *Disorders*). It depicts the sexual response in terms of three phases. The phases are desire, excitement, and orgasm. This is the model we will use to discuss the normal sexual response and in reviewing the topic of sexual dysfunction.

Sexual Desire

In most cases, married couples have sexual relations because of strong physical and emotional urges that are innately good and wholesome. Sexual desire "is the energy that allows an individual to initiate or respond to sexual stimulation," (ACOG Bulletin). Desire, or libido, is a complex phenomenon that is a by-product of a person's biology, past experiences, current marriage dynamics, and even spiritual factors. Low sexual desire is the most common sexual problem encountered in marriage.

EXCITEMENT

Sexual desire, when accompanied by stimulating sensations or memories, leads to sexual excitement, also called "arousal." The excitement phase is the second phase of the sexual response. Arousal results in predictable physiologic and anatomic changes, particularly of the genital tract, and is accompanied by sensations of pleasure. If sexual arousal is of sufficient duration and intensity, it culminates in orgasm.

When a husband and wife engage in sexual relations, they must first increase each other's level of arousal and prepare for intercourse through what is called "foreplay." This involves kissing, gentle touching of nonsexual areas of the body, and tender touching of sexually sensitive areas. Some people have used the terms "necking" and "petting" to describe these intimate physical activities among unmarried individuals, therefore, these terms often imply sinful conduct. But in marriage, this intimate contact is not only proper, it contributes significantly to sexual fulfillment.

For some couples, tender verbal exchanges and the sharing of personal feelings and expressions of love may enhance sexual arousal during foreplay, while others find that talking is a distraction. Ultimately, what is pleasurable to a given couple is unique to them and is a part of the sacred and private intimate life known only to the couple.

Sexual stimulation and arousal leads to anatomic changes in a carefully orchestrated interplay between the nervous, circulatory, and endocrine systems of the body. The physical changes are most noticeable in the genital area, but other areas of the body, such as the breasts, are affected as well. The primary physiologic event that occurs during sexual arousal is "vasocongestion." This literally means a "congestion of the blood vessels." During vasocongestion, the veins of the pelvis, including both blood vessels near the skin and vessels deep in the pelvic tissues, dilate and fill with blood. These vascular changes create enlargement of the genital organs and produce pleasant sensations of fullness and warmth.

In men, vasocongestion during sexual activity results in an increase in rigidity, length, and circumference of the penis. At the same time, the testes are drawn up closer to the body wall, and the genital area increases in sensitivity to touch. In women, vasocongestion leads to an enlargement, both in diameter and length, of the upper vaginal canal, and a narrowing or tightening of the lower vaginal canal. The uterus lifts into a higher position in the pelvic cavity and the vagina becomes lubricated through the creation of vaginal fluid. The labia swell and the clitoris increases in size and sensitivity. The breasts also enlarge in size and the nipples become erect and more sensitive to touch.

During sexual arousal, there is an increase in heart rate and deeper and more rapid breathing. Vasocongestion may also result in a flush or faint rash on the chest, neck, and face. Muscles of the genital area and throughout the body tighten in a process called myotonia. This causes the entire body to feel more sensitive to the touch.

The anatomic and physiologic changes associated with sexual arousal are accompanied by intense feelings of emotional and physical pleasure. As long as sexual stimulation is fairly constant and the individual is able to focus on the pleasant sensations he or she is feeling, the physical changes of arousal continue to take place. If the individual's attention is drawn away from the experience, as with a phone call or a crying baby, then sexual arousal will abate and the physical changes will reverse themselves.

INTERCOURSE AND ORGASM

During the excitement phase the genital organs become prepared for consummation of sexual union. The penis becomes erect and able to penetrate the vaginal canal. In turn, the vagina becomes lubricated, enlarged, and prepared to receive the penis. When both the husband and wife are ready, emotionally and physically, the penis is inserted into the vagina, and the couple moves rhythmically to maintain mutual stimulation. During this time, they may caress and talk to each other in loving ways. All of this provides continued stimulation and enjoyment and leads to the next phase of the sexual experience, orgasm.

Orgasm occurs when sexual arousal reaches a climax, or threshold. At that moment, all of the tension that has built up in the pelvis is suddenly released in a series of contractions involving the muscles of the internal and external sexual organs. Simultaneously, the blood that has collected in the pelvic veins is released to flow back into the body. Upon reaching orgasm, the wife experiences a series of involuntary rhythmic contractions of the muscles of the genital area. In the husband, orgasm results in ejaculation of semen in a series of similarly rhythmic contractions.

These contractions during orgasm produce remarkable feelings of intense pleasure. Only rarely, however, do the husband and wife reach this point of climax at the same time. Continued manual stimulation, maintaining and intensifying the level of arousal, will facilitate orgasm for the spouse. These extremely pleasurable sensations draw the married couple closer together and strengthen their emotional ties.

THE MYSTERY

In the area of human sexuality there is nothing more mysterious or widely discussed in the literature than orgasm. Much of the mystery surrounding orgasm stems from the intense pleasure associated with it, the wide variety of ways people perceive it, the fact that women have a more difficult time attaining it, and the emphasis it receives from many people as the most important aspect of the sexual experience. Perhaps a few comments about orgasm may be helpful:

- Not all people describe orgasm the same way. Some researchers think there may actually be different kinds of orgasm, but this is not well understood. However, no one should expect their orgasm to feel exactly like what someone else describes, especially since some descriptions of orgasm appear to be exaggerated.
- Orgasm is not perceived in the same way every time in every individual. It may be more or less intense, depending on many physical and psychological factors, such as how well a person is feeling or the quality of the relationship at the moment.
- Female orgasm may occur through clitoral stimulation alone, with vaginal penetration, or even on occasion by stimulation of the breasts. One way is not inherently superior to another.
- A man will usually achieve orgasm more easily and quickly than a woman. Male orgasm is the natural result of sustained arousal and stimulation of the penis.

- Orgasm is not the only purpose of sexual relations or the only route to sexual fulfillment. Additionally, it should not be the only goal of every sexual experience. Sexual intimacy can be fulfilling without orgasm. A person's ability to achieve orgasm changes according to a wide variety of physical and emotional factors, such as fatigue, mood, illness, and aging. Sometimes it occurs easily, other times it just doesn't happen.
- Neither the husband nor the wife should expect to achieve orgasm every time they have sexual relations, although the husband generally does so with more regularity than the wife. While some can experience more than one orgasm in a given sexual experience, this is relatively uncommon. Of those who can have multiple orgasms, it is much more common among women than men.

AFTERGLOW

Following orgasm, sexual arousal slowly abates. Some call this the afterglow period. Women remain sexually aroused following orgasm longer than men, which may explain why women seem to enjoy this time more than men. In the afterglow, the husband and wife may continue their embrace and bask in the emotions of the moment. Tender verbal exchanges and caresses continue, and it is a deeply satisfying time for most couples as they enjoy each other's closeness and reflect together on their affection and feelings.

During the afterglow period, the anatomic and physiologic changes that occurred during the excitement and orgasm phases reverse themselves, and the genital organs return to their previous unaroused state. The individuals then usually go through a period of time when another orgasm is not possible. This is called the refractory period, and its duration varies between individuals. It is generally longer for men than for women, and it increases in length as individuals age.

SUMMARY

The sexual experience for men and women is a wonderful, carefully orchestrated phenomenon involving several body systems and associated with intense emotions. From a biological perspective, its primary purpose is reproductive in nature, but in reality it also possesses significant psychological and spiritual dimensions. When all systems are healthy, sexual intimacy enriches the marital relationship. When marital, physical, or psychological problems are present, the joy of this union is diminished.

One of the great challenges surrounding the sexual experience relates to the fact that husbands and wives often have very different perspectives about sex. They may struggle to understand and respond to one another's needs and desires. They may have different expectations or may not know, or even care to know, how to make intimacy an enjoyable experience for their spouse. These differences can obviously create problems, but they can be overcome as the husband and wife work together to find the ways to provide a positive and fulfilling experience for one another.

CHAPTER 5

The Honeymoon

There are few days in one's life that are anticipated with as much excitement as the wedding day. It is usually a very joyous occasion, ripe with hope and promise. For most people, it represents the culmination of a lifetime of preparation. It is literally a "once in a lifetime" experience.

On their wedding day, the bride and groom experience a wide variety of emotions. They enjoy a sense of peace and solemnity as their two lives officially become one through the marriage ceremony. Of course, there is some understandable nervousness associated with that experience, but there is also gaiety and merriment in the post-wedding celebration as well-wishers gather to honor them. However, amidst the festivities of the day, both sacred and celebratory, there is often an unspoken undercurrent of apprehension on the part of the couple regarding what lies ahead. They wonder, "Will I know what to do when the time comes for sex? Will my spouse be patient with my uncertainties? Will it be a comfortable experience for both of us?"

When approached properly, most couples can rightly expect that their wedding night will be as enjoyable for them as they want it to be. However, for some couples the wedding night is not a pleasant experience and not one they remember with fondness. This happens for several reasons, including a lack of proper preparation and their own unrealistic expectations.

A few basic steps allow individuals to properly prepare themselves physically and emotionally for sexual intimacy on the honeymoon. Proper preparation helps each partner set realistic expectations and provides information that will help make the first sexual experience a positive one. This chapter reviews several ideas that couples can use to prepare themselves for marital intimacy in the first few days and weeks of marriage.

PLANNING

In general, preparation for the wedding day requires a great deal of advanced planning. Photos, catering, tuxedo rentals, a place for the reception, and a hundred other things have to be arranged. It takes an impressive amount of attention to detail and foresight to get it all done. Among all that must be accomplished in the months prior to marriage, however, the couple should not forget to prepare themselves for sexual intimacy. A few basic items can make the difference between an enjoyable honeymoon and a disaster.

Premarital Exam

It is important for the bride-to-be to have a gynecologic exam several months before the wedding date. The gynecologist can tell her if she should be able to consummate sexual relations without undue difficulty. The vast majority of women learn that everything is normal and that sexual intercourse can take place without any serious problems. Occasionally, however, the doctor may recommend dilation of the hymenal ring in order for sexual intercourse to proceed properly. Minor surgery to correct an anatomic problem is occasionally necessary. By having this exam several months before the wedding day, there will be sufficient time to get everything done—even if minor surgery is required.

Birth Control

Couples also need to decide how to handle the possibility of pregnancy. Ninety percent of couples will conceive within the first year of marriage if they do not use any birth control. If a couple decides to delay pregnancy, the premarital exam offers an opportunity to discuss birth control options with the gynecologist. Barrier forms of contraception such as condoms and diaphragms are often awkward for newlywed couples who are attempting sexual intercourse for the first time, and they are not as reliable as other methods. Hormonal forms of contraception, such as birth control pills or contraceptive injections, are generally easier and more effective for new couples, assuming there are no medical reasons that prevent their use. Optimally, these birth control methods should be started at least one month before the wedding date to make sure there are no side effects. Also, hormonal forms of contraception are not effective until they have been used for one month.

Intellectual Preparation

A certain amount of sex education before the wedding is also helpful. Reading a book about physical intimacy or discussing the topic with a parent or mentor has great value. As one young man said:

> *My wife and I were engaged for about five months. In that time we heard all kinds of advice about sex, everything from "don't discuss or study anything" to recommendations that we should have many frank discussions before marriage. We prayed about it and decided we would wait until a week before the big day to read about it. That way we had some knowledge, but didn't have it on our minds too far ahead. One of our parents gave us a book that answered a few of my major questions like what exactly should happen that first night and beyond. I quickly learned that there were many things I didn't know about physical intimacy.*

A young man and woman should not worry that they don't know everything about sex before marriage. One purpose of the honeymoon is to discover it together. It is normal and acceptable to have many questions about what lies ahead. Keep in mind that sexual intimacy in marriage is a journey, not a destination, and the discovery itself is a memorable part of the adventure. Recognizing this can help to diminish the anxiety that many couples experience as they anticipate the wedding night. However, some basic intellectual preparation in the immediate pre-wedding days can help avoid major problems that can arise in the first few weeks of marriage. As one young woman explained:

> *The night before my wedding, my parents sat me down and had a nice little talk with me about sex. I had also talked with my sister who had been married for a year and half. Because of these discussions, there was nothing uncomfortable about our wedding night. We each had an idea of what we wanted to have happen, and it did.*

Material used to prepare for marital intimacy should be of a wholesome nature, and as a rule, discussions between the engaged couple should be limited to general items. Usually, it is sufficient to simply reassure each other that both will do their best to make the experience as meaningful and enjoyable as possible. The details can be discussed later.

SUCCESSFUL HONEYMOON INTIMACY

Even though newlyweds normally do not know a lot about sexual intimacy, most of them do quite well. Most difficulties can be avoided if each partner looks after the welfare of his or her spouse, if there are realistic expectations about what will occur, and if both have a basic understanding of the male and female sexual response.

The Apostle Paul gave wonderful instructions on the kind of attitude that should exist in marriage. This applies to the total relationship, but is also specifically applicable to intimacy. He said: "Husbands, love your wives, even as Christ also loved the church, and gave himself for it. . . . So ought men to love their wives as their own bodies. He that loveth his wife loveth himself," (Eph. 5:23–25, 28). In order for both partners to enjoy the honeymoon, there must be a spirit of love, concern, patience, and tenderness. There should be a sensitivity to each other's feelings and a sincere desire to help each other find fulfillment in the sexual experience. There is no place for selfishness or personal gratification.

It is helpful for a couple to know that most men experience a more powerful sex drive than women; they become sexually aroused more quickly, and it is usually easier for them to reach orgasm. They should also know that, although women possess an equal, if not greater, desire for emotional, social, and physical intimacy, they do not necessarily desire sexual consummation with the same intensity or frequency as men.

Since orgasm does not occur as easily for women, the husband and wife may need to learn together how to make it possible. Female orgasm usually requires concentration and effort. It also requires that the woman be fairly comfortable with the sexual experience. For this reason, orgasm usually comes more easily as the relationship matures, but sometimes it can take years to achieve. One woman shared her experience:

> *After a couple weeks of being married, my husband and I went looking for a book to help us. I had not climaxed yet and this was perplexing to my husband. After we were intimate together, he wanted to analyze my problem. He blamed himself and told me he just couldn't satisfy me. I really began to dislike making love because I knew that I wouldn't climax and then my husband would be unhappy. Plus, it was frustrating to not climax. There was just so much pressure.*

A young husband tells a similar story:

> *One thing that was frustrating to me was the female orgasm. I had read a lot about how different it was for her than for me, that it isn't as automatic, but I really didn't know what to expect. I really wanted my wife to experience an orgasm the first time we had sex. Unfortunately, it didn't happen. My wife explained she was too scared and tense. Later into our marriage she was finally able to fully enjoy sex with an orgasm. She has learned how to concentrate on her feelings and sensations and she is now able to experience orgasm much more easily.*

These newlywed couples struggled early in their sexual experiences because of unrealistic expectations. A woman does not normally experience orgasm early in the sexual relationship. So if it does not happen, it should not be a cause for worry.

COMMUNICATION

The importance of talking together, sharing information, and instructing each other cannot be overemphasized. Each spouse should openly share his or her needs and wants, not only in the first few days of marriage, but throughout their life together. Each partner should regularly inquire, in a sensitive way, how the spouse feels and what can be done to help the companion find greater joy and fulfillment in the sexual experience.

Talking about sex is not always easy for newlyweds to do. A young woman said,

> One of the things that was initially difficult early in our marriage was talking about our likes and dislikes regarding physical intimacy. It took some time to learn what each of us enjoyed. In order to do this we had to talk about what we liked and disliked. This was often awkward because it was new territory for us. But it was so helpful for me.

Good communication helps marriage partners learn what works best in their particular situation. One husband put it this way:

> When we are intimate, we talk with each other and guide each other verbally and nonverbally in the process. By doing so, we are able to more fully enjoy the experience together. Communication is necessary because my wife and I may not always be in the same mood as each other. Sometimes the approach needs to be changed due to a mood swing or preference. Communication helps this to happen in the most appropriate way.

In an attempt to be sensitive to the feelings of his spouse, a man can end up placing undo pressure on his wife by regularly asking whether or not she has reached climax. While the man's concern is commendable, it can make a woman feel pressured to respond or to perform according to his expectations. Clear communication can be the key to ensuring that both husband and wife enjoy the experience in the way that is comfortable and fulfilling for each.

COMMENTS ABOUT THE HONEYMOON

A primary purpose of the honeymoon is to enjoy the emotions and feelings of physical closeness. It is a time of mutual sexual exploration and discovery. For most people, it is a wonderful beginning to a lifetime of marital intimacy. However, in any gathering of women, if the subject of the honeymoon comes up, there are a few who admit, either to themselves or openly, that their initial experiences were not good. This is frequently due to the fact that they had difficulty consummating sexual intercourse the first few times. This may have been due to pain or an inability to relax enough to allow intercourse to take place. Here are a variety of comments from newlyweds who talked about their experiences:

- *Something I had a difficult time with was the discomfort, or pain, that I felt with the first episode of intercourse. My gynecologist said that I was small and that sex would probably be uncomfortable, but uncomfortable was an understatement. I had talked to my husband about my premarital exam and told him that sex would probably be very uncomfortable for me, and I was glad I did. I was so grateful that I had an understanding husband who was gentle and was concerned about my feelings. Perhaps, if he hadn't known about my situation, he would have behaved in a manner that could have caused me a lot of physical and emotional pain.*

- *That first night was a very interesting one. It didn't seem right to talk about it before we were married because of the taboo nature of the subject. And so the first night, my wife and I had very different expectations, and things did not turn out exactly as either of us expected.*

- *I was very happy to find out what a patient husband I married. I was quite nervous about the pain that everybody told me about when having sex for the first time. He was very understanding and sweet about the whole thing.*

- *I didn't have much preparation for the pain and discomfort involved. I came into marriage extremely naive about sexual relations. But what I experienced that first night was not only quite a surprise, it was also the most beautifully bonding experience I had ever shared.*

- *At first I wasn't very interested in sex, but I certainly didn't want to reject my husband. It was pretty scary when I first saw how passionate he could get. That was a new experience for me, and it was pretty one-sided for awhile.*

- *One thing I wish I had known about sex before our honeymoon is that it takes practice to get it right and feel comfortable. On my honeymoon, I had imagined a night full of intimacy like you see on television. I thought my wife and I would absolutely love it and it would be lots of fun. However, things didn't turn out as I expected. After trying intercourse several times, we failed. In fact, for the next two weeks, we tried every night to have intercourse, but without success. We have been married about three months now, and we are just beginning to have sex without my wife feeling so much pain. I wish I would have known before I got married that this might happen.*

FEMALE PROBLEMS

Women usually have pain with their first episodes of intercourse. This occurs because of an anatomical structure called the hymen. The hymen is a membrane or ring of skin that partially covers the vaginal opening. The first time sexual intercourse is undertaken, it is normal for there to be stretching and tearing of the hymenal skin. This can cause mild discomfort or, in some cases, severe pain. Bleeding can occur as well.

Even from birth, all hymens are not the same. Some women have very little hymenal tissue, while others have near-complete blockage of the vaginal opening by a thick band of tissue. This means that some women have very little difficulty with their first sexual experience, while others may have significant problems. Obviously, if a problem is not discovered until the honeymoon, there will be pain, frustration, and embarrassment for the couple as they try to engage in their first sexual experience together. This underscores the need for an exam before marriage to detect and treat potential problems. When needed, physicians can explain to prospective brides some exercises that allow them to dilate the hymenal opening and prepare for sexual consummation.

A personal lubricant can be very helpful for many couples, particularly during their first few sexual experiences. These products can be purchased in most pharmacies. Lubricants will allow penile penetration to occur with greater ease and less pain for the woman. A pain reliever taken about an hour before intercourse may also help to avoid or alleviate discomfort. Consummation of sexual intercourse requires that the woman relax, and that her husband proceed slowly and gently. Any tensing of the muscles of the vaginal opening can make penetration difficult.

MALE PROBLEMS

Honeymoon difficulties are not limited to women. Not uncommonly, men have difficulty obtaining an erection or delaying ejaculation until the penis has penetrated the vaginal opening. Two new husbands shared the following experiences:

- *About two weeks after we were married, I was getting very frustrated with myself because my wife wasn't reaching a climax. It was worrying me so much that I couldn't perform. Sometimes I couldn't get an erection, or I would lose it. This just complicated matters more. I finally had to stop fretting over my wife not reaching a climax, because it was just making matters worse.*

- *Our first nights together were much different than I had anticipated. I was very nervous that I wouldn't do everything right, so much so that it affected what I was able to do. The stress*

was killing me. It took my wife's calming influence, telling me
we had an eternity to practice, to make me patient enough to
be able to control my body. It took us quite a few times to
actually complete the union. Since then things have just kept
getting better.

PRACTICE MAKES PERFECT

World class athletes often comment that they perform their best
when they let the game come to them, rather than trying to force
their presence and influence on the game. This approach is appropriate for sexual intimacy, as well. The experience cannot be forced.
Take it as it comes, be patient, and with time each partner will grow
in his or her enjoyment and fulfillment. One newlywed said,

> *I didn't know that it takes practice and the first time and*
> *many times after that it won't be that great. I was expecting*
> *perfect sex on the first night. It didn't quite happen that way. I*
> *didn't know that if a couple didn't have great sex the first night*
> *that nothing is wrong with them and that with practice things*
> *will go much better. It just takes a little time and patience.*

WEDDING DAY BLUES

A couple of other ideas may be considered when planning the
honeymoon. Wedding days are typically exhausting, both physically
and emotionally. Not only is there the marriage ceremony itself, but
the bride and groom are also the center of attention at the post-
wedding festivities. Often this includes a brunch or luncheon and a
reception or open house. In addition, there may be many miles of
travel to the site of the wedding and to the reception. This makes for
a very weary couple at the end of the day and may set the stage for
disappointment that night. One wife made this point:

> *We got married in December a few days after final exams.*
> *After a hectic month of school, work, apartment shopping,*
> *packing, moving, unpacking, cleaning, traveling, and a long*
> *weekend of wedding festivities, by the time we got to our hotel*

*room on our wedding night we were so tired I wanted to fall
over and go to sleep for a week. We both wanted to enjoy our
first intimate night together, but we were so tired we didn't
take time to do it right. We just ended up frustrated, upset,
and even more tired than before. What a disaster that week
was.*

One solution may be to move some of the less important festivities to a day other than the wedding day. Some people even move the reception to the night before the wedding. That way, as soon as the post-wedding luncheon is over, the couple is free to set out on their honeymoon. Some couples prefer to get married on a weekday and have the reception on the weekend, when they are more rested and less nervous.

Finally, there is the idea of "gradual intimacy" or a delayed honeymoon. One recent bride told what they did:

*Although the questions I had about sex were being
addressed through discussions with my parents, I was still a
little scared for the honeymoon. I just couldn't fathom how one
minute I was expected to stay as far away from sexual intimacy as possible, then as soon as we'd say our "I do's," BOOM!
Sex was legal! Luckily I had a sister who had a little discussion
with us. Her counsel to us was this: don't feel pressured to have
sex your first night together. She recommended "gradual intimacy." For some reason, we couldn't schedule our honeymoon
until several weeks after we were married. I am glad we didn't
take our wedding trip until then! After several weeks of getting
to know each other physically, we were ready to enjoy our
honeymoon together as a relaxed husband and wife. We thor-
oughly enjoyed our time together that week.*

Bladder Infections

Women often return from their honeymoon with bladder infections, known in medical circles as "honeymoon cystitis." The symptoms include painful and frequent urination or blood in the urine. Bladder infections are caused by bacterial contamination of the urethra and bladder that occurs during sexual intercourse.

Unfortunately, when long honeymoons are taken, the couple may find themselves in a distant city or country when the symptoms of the infection begin. This can require the wife to go to a clinic or be seen by a doctor in a place far from home, which may be embarrassing, time consuming, and expensive, to say nothing of disrupting the honeymoon plans.

Several things can be done to avoid bladder infections. The first is for the wife to urinate soon after intercourse. This empties the bladder of any bacteria that may have traveled there during sexual activity. The second is to drink fluids, particularly juices that acidify the urine. This prevents bacteria from growing in the bladder. Cranberry juice is an example of an acidic juice. The third suggestion is to carry a small supply of antibiotics if prolonged travel is planned. In this way, medical help will already be in hand if symptoms should arise. This topic can be addressed with the gynecologist at the time of the premarital exam.

ADDITIONAL SUGGESTIONS

- Although there is no medical risk, couples may find it uncomfortable to have sexual intercourse during the woman's menstrual period. Where possible, the wedding date should be scheduled at a time when the woman is not menstruating. If the woman is planning to take birth control pills, the gynecologist can work with her to change the date of her expected menses, if necessary. This needs to be arranged with the doctor at least four weeks before the wedding date.

- Many people are naturally modest. They may be uncomfortable about being seen without clothing. If this is the case, the room lighting can be adjusted to make each partner comfortable. In time, the shyness diminishes.

- People wonder about what to do about garments during sexual relations. We advise people to remember their temple covenants and the counsel they received regarding their use. Certain activities obviously require their removal, including swimming and some athletic events. Each couple should discuss this matter together to determine how to best handle this issue.

- People have related questions regarding the wearing of lingerie or negligees during intimate activity. Again, this is a decision that a husband and wife make together.
- Some people carry unresolved guilt because of past sexual sins. This prevents them from fully enjoying marital intimacy. Complete repentance should allow for guilt-free sexual relations in marriage. If feelings of guilt persist despite repentance, this should be discussed with the appropriate ecclesiastical leader.
- Some people have problems enjoying intimacy in marriage because of past sexual abuse. Of course, one may not know whether this will be an issue until sexual intimacy is attempted. However, if sexual abuse has occurred, it may be wise to discuss the issue ahead of time. The assistance of a counselor may be helpful in this matter.

CHAPTER 6

What I Wish I'd Known

A number of married students, most of whom had been married fewer than two years, talked about their experiences with physical intimacy as honeymooners. They reflected back on what they knew (and what they wish they had known) about this topic before marriage. What problems could they have avoided through better preparation? Is it possible to prepare anyone for physical relations beforehand? Or, is the excitement and anticipation of discovering their sexuality together more important than "knowing all" before marriage? There were a variety of responses. Some felt their parents had cheated them by not discussing the topic of intimacy clearly enough, while others felt that the only person who could have helped them adjust to physical intimacy was their spouse.

> *I think there are so many of these darn "prude families" that will say nothing about intimacy to their children, like it's something dirty. Of course we should abstain before marriage, but there are so many women (and men, but probably a lot fewer) that have a hard time with sex when they get married because they feel it is something bad. I believe too many youth are not correctly informed about sex. I know when I got engaged I really wanted to know what was going to happen other than how the pieces fit together. My mom is a nurse, and*

she gave me some of the medical side of sex. But she also gave me this important counsel: "Just enjoy being with your husband. Enjoy doing something that only the two of you share, and remember that you couldn't show your love for each other in any stronger, sweeter, and more powerful way. Of course it will take a while before you two know what you are doing." I felt that she told me just enough without giving it all away and I love her for it!

The average young person hears a number of firesides and discussions on the "evils of sexual involvement" before marriage. Then, at marriage, the new couple is expected to somehow flip a psychological switch and suddenly be fully prepared for sex. This lack of preparation presents challenges to many newly married couples.

It is very awkward to one day have everything off limits and then the next day be able to actually have sexual relations. My wife told me that part of the problem she had was not knowing what to expect, but at the same time she did not think it was proper to ask others about it. We didn't know how much we could talk about sex before we got married, and so we ended up not talking about it at all. If engaged couples were given some realistic help and counsel as to what to expect, then they would be much better prepared to be intimate partners.

A wife of a few years expressed these sentiments:

I believe that couples about to enter into marriage should be counseled more explicitly on what is proper conduct in their sexual relationship. It seems strange that a girl is taught all her life that the way a young man shows respect to her is by not touching her. Then after a half hour ceremony, some cake and punch, and cheery goodbyes from parents, everything has changed. Now she is to give her body and soul to a man she may have known less than a year!

I married a righteous young man, but we were both so programmed from Standard Nights that we had a hard time touching each other without feeling guilty. I wasn't sure he

*respected me after our wedding night and he wasn't sure about
me either. We also wondered what was acceptable behavior
now that we were married. He wasn't sure if I should touch
him when he needed help becoming aroused because of all his
past training. I honestly didn't know any more than he did.*

*Our introduction to intimacy occurred when we both met
with my gynecologist for a premarital exam. His advice was so
explicit that it scared us and we didn't try it out until years
later. This was unfortunate because he gave us some good
counsel. He explained that female arousal takes longer than
male arousal, and he offered advice to help us both enjoy the
experience. For the first few years, I only enjoyed sex because it
made my husband happy.*

Here's another reaction:

*The world has gone overboard discussing and portraying
inappropriate sex and intimacy. On the other hand, most of us
grew up thinking that sex was some huge secret we were not
supposed to talk about or think about. But how can teenagers
who are just discovering these new developments in their own
bodies not think about it? I understand that with too much
explicit information, vulnerable teens are curious, but if it
weren't seen as such a taboo subject, maybe teens would be less
curious. We need to help teens understand the consequences,
but not make it a topic that can never be discussed or thought
about.*

A newly married wife felt this way:

*The way you teach your children about sexual intimacy
will make all the difference in their attitudes towards sex. My
parents were hesitant to address the topic of physical intimacy.
As a result, I was scared of it. On the other hand, my
husband's parents were completely open with him about sex.
His attitude towards physical intimacy was positive and much
more healthy than mine. I know that we could do a much
better job teaching our families that sexual intimacy is a
special, sacred "sacrament" between a man and a woman—*

and the Lord should be included. He intended these relation-
ships to be meaningful to each companion within the bounds
of marriage.

Although parents have the responsibility to teach their children
about sexual matters, some mothers and fathers do not do much in
the way of providing specific information or help. Many seem to
expect their children to approach them with their questions. But if
parents appear intimidated, embarrassed, or scandalized by the
subject, what child will feel comfortable coming to them for information or counsel?

> *I have pondered many times the question of how and*
> *when to talk about sex to my own children some day. I did*
> *have the "birds and the bees" talk when I was younger, but I*
> *really don't remember much except for thinking, "Weird."*
> *When and from whom are we to learn how to have proper*
> *and "sacramental" sex? My mother tried to explain to me that*
> *sex was a beautiful and holy thing, but from what I had expe-*
> *rienced in my high school years, seeing a few movies and*
> *running across some magazines as a young boy, I had pictured*
> *it as ugly, sinful, and selfish. When I thought of how I came to*
> *be, I knew that Mom and Dad must have done something,*
> *but it definitely wasn't what I had seen or heard about, and*
> *they must have done it just because they wanted a family. They*
> *almost never talked about sex; in fact they never even kissed in*
> *front of us.*
> *Growing up in the Church, we are often told what not to*
> *do, but when do we learn what is appropriate and good in*
> *marriage? If we don't ever learn about what is permissible,*
> *how are we supposed to know? Dad always said he would give*
> *me the talk, so the night before we were married, he took me*
> *on a walk and said, "Son, you know all the things you were*
> *told not to do before, well, now you're supposed to do them."*
> *He mentioned that I should go slowly, that guys can be ready*
> *in a moment, but a wife needed some time. My wife and I*
> *learned through experience that the "time" needed is really the*
> *time for her to develop some lubrication so that it can be*
> *comfortable for her. How many people knew that? I didn't.*

We suggested earlier that engaged couples should wait until just before marriage to discuss the details of their impending sexual relationship. However, parents should take the opportunity to discuss with their children how to make sex a positive and uplifting aspect of married life. This discussion need not address techniques or details. In fact, a few calm and honest words about the purposes of sex, its role within the overall relationship, and some basic information on male and female physiology can help to establish principles that will allow the young couple to discover together how to proceed. General guidelines about making sex a positive experience for the spouse or learning to communicate openly about intimacy will be far more useful than descriptions of what is or is not appropriate. As the young person approaches marriage, a bishop or medical doctor may be able to offer additional help and counsel. Doing so could have saved this couple some difficulties:

> *If two people who have never really been exposed to sex get married, and they don't know what to do—in fact, months go by and they are getting frustrated because she hasn't had an orgasm, where do they go to learn what they can do? Where does a couple learn how to have an appropriate and fulfilling sexual relationship? Ideally they talk it through, but what if they don't really know what it is they are trying to accomplish? For example, what does an orgasm feel like for a woman? If she feels really good, is that it?*

PREPARING FOR THE FIRST INTIMATE EXPERIENCE

As we indicated previously, most couples come into marriage with a sincere desire to please each other. Yet, if they have been chaste, they know almost nothing about how to approach sex in a way that will be fulfilling to the spouse other than what they may have read or what a friend or relative may have shared. The spirit of adventure, discovery, and learning must exist as a couple begins this part of their experience together.

> *On our wedding night, my husband had no idea how to get me ready for intimacy, and honestly, I didn't really know*

what I needed either. He thought I would take one look at him, melt into his arms, and that would be it. It sure would have made things a whole lot easier that night if women were as easy to arouse as men, but it doesn't quite happen that way. Since we were so inexperienced at this, my husband concluded that I just didn't want to have sex with him and that's why I wasn't getting aroused. He wondered if I really loved him. We eventually just went to sleep that night, tired and frustrated.

Often honeymoons are not as successful as we assume they will be. A healthy and enjoyable sexual relationship does not develop easily for many new couples. But usually they can, with patience and thoughtfulness, overcome inhibitions and learn to find joy together in this newly developing aspect of their lives.

I wish I had known about the importance of foreplay— especially in preparing a new bride who has never had sex for that first experience with intimacy. We laugh about it now, but I felt like a selfish, abusive husband after our first experience as my wife began to cry from pain. I had no idea it would hurt her like that, and she was not really prepared for it either. If anything will open the gates of communication, pain will. Over the ensuing months, we talked a lot about what our bodies need and what our expectations were.

Many of these young couples felt they were unprepared for intimacy when they married. Some wished they had received better instruction from parents and Church leaders. But how specific should leaders be about sexual activities?

The main reason Church leaders don't discuss the specifics of what is appropriate in marriage is not because they are ashamed or don't want to give anyone new ideas, but rather because they feel the importance of teaching correct principles and letting the members govern themselves. Although they may never discuss the nitty-gritty of sexual intimacy, they will never cease to talk about the importance of seeking the Spirit in marriage. This leaves the answers to specific questions for couples to learn through the gifts of the Holy Ghost and agency. While some may find this frustrating, this is really Heavenly Father's way of teaching the people to seek after Him.

The Lord has told us that is "not meet that [He] should command in all things," (D&C 58:26). Thankfully, He has also said: "If any of you lack wisdom, let him ask of God, that giveth to all men liberally, and upbraideth not; and it shall be given him," (James 1:5). To some these two scriptures may seem contradictory, but they are actually complementary. The closer a couple draws to one another and to the Lord, the more they realize that sexual intimacy is only one small, but important, facet of married life. As they begin to see and treat each other as the King or Queen they are, the questions, fears, and apprehensions they once faced will turn into strengths, powers, and a solid bond that will grow and flourish throughout eternity. As they find the answers to their questions by seeking the Lord's guidance and helping each other, they will truly be unified as a couple.

Parents and leaders need to help youth understand this important fact: when a man and woman have entered into sacred covenants with God to help each other come unto Him, sexual relations provide a marvelous way to invigorate and strengthen that relationship. If young people preparing for marriage can comprehend that sex will help them draw closer to God as they set aside selfishness and seek to build greater unity with their spouse, they will be better prepared to recognize and respect appropriate boundaries. One young woman put it this way:

I have thought about the principle of listening to the Spirit in order to discern what is right and wrong sexually. Unfortunately, I believe that far too many of us are not in tune with the Spirit enough to be able to hear its whisperings when we do something wrong—especially when we deal with something so emotional and hormonal. Many of us do not even give a thought to the Spirit in our marital intimate relationships. I feel very blessed that many of the intimate times I have shared with my husband have been of a spiritual nature.

I have felt the Spirit testifying to me that what we were doing as a couple was right and proper. Sometimes we mislead our youth to suppose that anything that is sexual, is evil.

Summary

Marital intimacy is a great adventure for new couples joining hands and hearts and bodies for the first time. As Latter-day Saints, we are hesitant to provide too much information to young couples for fear that they might experiment before marriage. On the other hand, sometimes couples have unrealistic expectations and are disappointed when they find discrepancies between what they had anticipated and what actually happens. There is a fine line between what a young couple needs to know before the marriage and what might be too suggestive. The principles taught must be candid enough to explain what is right and wrong in sexual matters without becoming graphic or titillating. Hopefully, wise parents and ecclesiastical leaders can discern that line as they counsel youth in preparation for the intimate expressions of love and affection within marriage. We want our youth to anticipate marital intimacy as a wonderful experience.

CHAPTER 7

About Men and Women

Dave had been married to Laura for three years. She was a university graduate working at a local bank, and he was still in college. When they married, Dave really thought he had found his dream girl. She was beautiful, talented, and fun to be around. He was sure he'd be happy for the rest of his life. But now, he privately wondered whether his marriage would survive. What was their problem? He was almost embarrassed to think about it, but it was sex. Their sexual differences had driven a wedge between them, and he didn't know what to do.

Laura had been raised in what most people would consider a good home. Her parents were kind people, although intensely private. She never saw them express any outward signs of affection. Sexual matters were not mentioned in the home; they were simply off-limits. The message was, "we don't discuss those kinds of issues here."

Dave grew up in a very different kind of home. His parents were openly affectionate and very demonstrative. In addition, he shared a bathroom with three brothers. Being naked around them was no big deal. His family just had a more open approach to sex and nudity.

Dave and Laura were not prepared to deal with their different attitudes toward sex when they got married, mostly because they didn't realize they had different attitudes. They had never discussed sex, and their wedding night was a disappointing experience. Laura had never been told what to expect, and she was very uncomfortable with their first attempts at sexual intimacy. This was also new territory for Dave, but while Dave eventually became more comfortable with marital intimacy and enjoyed it, sex continued to be unpleasant for Laura. She wanted to be a good wife, but as hard as she tried, she could not relax and enjoy sex. Over time, she came to hate it and avoided it whenever possible.

Their difference in sexual attitudes eventually became the source of repeated disagreements and hurtful feelings. Laura couldn't understand why sex was so important to Dave. Did he really love her, or was he just interested in her for sex? At the same time, Dave couldn't understand why his wife didn't want to be intimate. Why was she so prudish? Why did she push him away? Their differences had driven them apart, and they were uncertain how to resolve the problem. Privately, Dave wondered if their marriage would make it. What were they to do?

A COMMON SCENARIO

Unfortunately, this is not an uncommon scenario. It is estimated that more than half of all couples experience significant sexual problems at some point in their marriage. These problems can threaten the entire relationship. As noted previously, President Spencer W. Kimball stated:

> Divorces often occur over sex, money, and child discipline. If you study the divorces, as we have had to do in these past years, you will find there are one, two, three, four reasons. Generally sex is the first. They did not get along sexually. They may not say that in the court. They may not even tell that to their attorneys, but that is the reason. Husband and wife . . . are authorized, in fact they are commanded, to have proper sex when they are properly married for time and eternity. (Kimball, *Teachings*, 329.)

Sadly, strained feelings over sex can become a private, silent wedge in a marriage. In some cases, sexual problems weaken an otherwise wonderful relationship or become a source of repeated, hurtful arguments and painful barbs.

Of course, dissatisfaction with the sexual relationship in marriage does not always result in divorce. There are many couples who feel their marriage meets their general expectations, except in the area of sexual intimacy. Most of these couples stay together because they really do love each other (Hammond, "Sex Therapy," 14). If they could, however, they would gladly change things about their sex lives. They simply don't know how.

DIFFERENCES

Many times the differences between husband and wife are not discovered until after marriage. One woman made this observation: "I think it is very important for girls to realize that sex means two different things to a male and female. Women are more romantic and men are more physical."

Differences in attitudes may not cause much concern in other aspects of marriage, but an individual can only find sexual fulfillment with the cooperation of a willing, sensitive, and compatible spouse. One of the most common complaints brought up with marriage counselors has to do with spouses who are not willing to make sex a good experience for their partner. We often hear, "He (or she) doesn't understand my needs and where I'm coming from and doesn't seem to want to."

If husbands and wives are to enjoy marital intimacy, it is vital for them to know as much as they can about each other's attitudes and feelings, and accommodate for differences. It is often helpful to know how the opposite gender perceives sex. However, before we talk about male and female characteristics, it should be emphasized that the following descriptions are, at best, generalizations. Not all men, or all women, see sex the same way. For example, it is well known that the sex drive is usually stronger among men than among women, but this is not always the case. In some marriages, the opposite is true. Also, contrary to sex-role stereotypes, there are situations where a wife is more comfortable with sexual matters and initiates intimate activity more often than the husband.

Sex Drive

With sexual problems, the greatest source of conflict in marriages relates to differences in sexual desire. Generally speaking, the sex drive is higher in men than in women. This is largely due to the influence of testosterone on the male brain. Short-term differences in libido are not a serious problem. However, if there is a significant difference in sex drive over a long period of time, it usually becomes an issue of concern in the marriage. One woman said,

> As is usually the case, my husband wanted sex more often than I did, but because he would either suggest or request sex often, I began to want it less and less, and we ended up having it only when I asked for it. This did not please him or me. We finally had a discussion on the topic, and we now have a mutual understanding. He understands that I do not want sex every time he does, and I am more willing to be intimate for his sake, even though I may not want it. This way we are both able to enjoy intimacy.

Another major distinction between most men and women is the different emphasis they place on sex in the relationship. It has been said, "Men give love to get sex; women give sex to get love." While this overstates the case, men and women do seem to understand sex quite differently. One woman shared her experience:

> My husband equates love with sex. I equate love with being allowed to sleep. He would become enraged when I turned him down in the bedroom. He became angry with me, and started treating me with hostility. I felt used, like I was unloved and abandoned. We had petty arguments over how many times a week we should be intimate. I began to hate that aspect of our life. If he decided to shave at night, I began to dread our encounter. I stayed up late watching TV to avoid a confrontation in the bedroom, and I doubted his motives when he showed kindness to me.

Men often have difficulty with the fact that their wives are less interested in sexual intimacy than they are. One new husband said,

> I was heartbroken the night I asked her what was wrong and she said, "I just don't want to make love tonight." It didn't

*matter that I knew that she loved me, I still felt like she loved
me less that night. I have since learned to accept the fact that
her expression of love is not as physical as mine, and I have
tried to change how I show her love to match her needs.*

The male ego can be rather fragile in this regard. Men frequently
experience a sense of rejection when their wives are not interested in
sexual intimacy. A husband will commonly interpret his wife's disin-
terest as a personal insult, showing insensitivity to his desires and
belittling his virility. On the other hand, women often have difficulty
understanding why their husbands want so much sex and why they
are not content just being close. They feel used and unappreciated.
Clear and considerate communication between husband and wife can
help them find an acceptable balance where each feels comfortable
and respects the emotions of the other.

SEXUAL CUES

Another difference between men and women has to do with how
they respond to varying sexual cues. Advertisers spend millions of
dollars each year on marketing that capitalizes on the fact that sex
sells. They use sexual images to sell everything from cars to razors.
This is because people, particularly men, are influenced by these
messages. But these images, which are intended to affect a person's
buying habits, can also influence sexual attitudes and behavior in a
marriage. Men are typically prone to respond to such visual stimuli
with heightened sexual desire. Whether processed on a conscious level
or subconsciously, this imagery can generate a physiological response
in the viewer, affecting hormone production and influencing mood.
A billboard message noticed on the drive home from work can subtly
increase a husband's interest in being sexually intimate with his wife
that night.

On the other hand, women are more apt to experience an increase
in sexual desire in response to emotional cues, such as genuine tenderness or a thoughtful word or deed. And women's sex drives are more
likely to be negatively influenced by external factors such as stress.
Whereas a man's interest in sexual matters is relatively strong and
consistent, with only moderate ups and downs, a woman's sex drive

often swings from one extreme to the other and more easily shifts with her moods. If the bills aren't paid, if the house is a mess, if there has been an argument, or if there is anything that upsets the wife's emotional equilibrium, her sex drive can be negatively affected. This also occurs with certain physical conditions, such as pregnancy or the premenstrual phase of the ovulatory cycle. Conversely, a romantic movie that reaches her emotionally can increase her desire for physical intimacy.

The need to understand the connection between mood and desire, and to respect differences, was well-expressed by one woman who said,

> It is important for my husband to realize that I might not always be in the mood for physical intimacy. He needs to respect this. I am not saying this only from a woman's point of view. I know that my husband wants to make love more frequently than I do, but there are also times when I would like it, and he is reluctant for whatever reason. Part of marriage is sacrifice—we need to love our spouse more than ourselves. Sometimes we also need to help fulfill each other's needs—even if we are not in the mood.

Approaches to Intimacy

Women find fulfillment through nonsexual physical contact more readily than men. A woman may frequently prefer a tender embrace, a romantic walk, or a gentle caress, without the expectation that it will lead to sex. One husband shared his experience:

> One of the most difficult things for me to understand in our marriage is that if we don't have sex we can still be intimate. I have a real hard time when I initiate something and my wife doesn't feel up to it. It is not that she doesn't love me, or want to be involved, but it just isn't a good time for her. Well, even though she tells me these things, I still feel rejected. Then she wants me to snuggle up to her and hold her and whisper sweet nothings in her ear. For her, it is security and intimacy. For me, it's rejection. But she's helping me learn that

> *I can enjoy being physically intimate with her even when I know we will not necessarily go all the way.*

When it comes to sexual activity itself, men often want to rush through the experience faster than women. Women need more time for arousal. Countless stories could be told of men who don't understand their wives' need to go slowly and take their time. They ignorantly assume that because they are aroused and ready for sex, their wives are too. Next to dealing with differences in sex drive, this is one of the most frequent complaints women voice regarding their sexual experiences.

Fortunately, a husband can learn, but he has to be taught. His wife must serve as the tutor. This requires communication, patience, and understanding. On this subject one wife advised,

> *Don't be shy about discussing your wants and feelings. Things got better when we overcame our shyness and began to discuss our feelings. It helps to talk about what feels good. Your husband can't read your mind. Your body is somewhat of a mystery to him. Sexual intimacy is better when he understands your likes and dislikes.*

Women are often more sensitive to relationship problems and more expressive about their feelings. They are also more apt to say what they are thinking and feeling. However, as previously noted, men sometimes interpret their wives' comments as criticism or rejection. The art of communication requires thoughtful care on both sides.

WHY ARE WE SO DIFFERENT?

It may be helpful to understand why a husband and wife are so different. No two people, even of the same sex, possess exactly the same innate personality, genetic makeup, and set of life experiences. Consequently, every person has his or her own sexual identity: a unique set of sexual ideas, feelings, desires, attitudes, expectations, and needs. Marriage represents, among other things, the uniting of two unique sexual identities into one lifetime relationship, a merging of each person's accumulated attitudes and characteristics.

Since no two individuals are exactly alike, there are sure to be differences regarding sexual matters between spouses. These may manifest themselves in a variety of different ways, including the emphasis placed on sex, how often sexual activity is desired, and how each responds to sexual cues. These differences must be accounted for in the relationship. In fact, the degree to which a couple discovers their shared similarities, and resolves their differences, largely determines the success or failure of their sexual relationship.

Sexual Identity

An individual's sexual identity is a composite of a complex set of influences. There are two points of view about how a person's sexual characteristics are determined. One is that sexual identity is strictly a product of nature. That is, an individual's genetic makeup and biology determine sexual behavior and attitudes. The second position is that sexual identity is a result of nurture or the environment in which a person is reared. There are very strong arguments to support each viewpoint.

Biological Influences

It is well known that biological influences shape an individual's sexual anatomy and physiology. For example, whether an individual is a male or female is determined by the genetic code inside the cells. In a fairly well-understood process, the X and Y chromosomes send signals that determine whether male or female sexual anatomy is formed. Gender is the single most important biological determinant of sexual identity. But chromosomes do much more than determine gender and external anatomy. They also indirectly determine the kind of brain that develops in a particular individual.

Researchers have established that the brains of men and women are not exactly the same. Certain areas of the brain, which some experts call sex centers, don't look or function the same in men and women at all—they are distinctly different. These differences can be seen as early as the fetal stage and are believed to be due primarily to the effect of testosterone, which bathes the male brain during early development. Simply put, if testosterone is present, a male brain is formed; if it is absent, a female brain develops. The further release of testosterone at the time of puberty activates the male sex centers, leading to physical development and exerting a strong influence upon men's attitudes and behaviors.

Environmental Influences

Many life events from early childhood through adulthood also shape a person's sexual identity. It has been shown that a child's sense of gender, that is, whether he or she identifies himself or herself as a male or female, is determined before age three. A person's sense of gender role, or how he or she should act based upon gender, is established by age five. This means that a child already understands what his or her sex is and how persons of that sex are supposed to behave before starting kindergarten.

Relationships also shape sexual identity. Generally, the single most important relationship in a child's life, and the one that molds his or her sense of sexual-self the most, is the parent-child relationship. Through instruction and example, a parent teaches a child how to behave consistent with socially accepted gender stereotypes. The influence of parents continues to be strong throughout a child's life, although once adolescence is reached, peer influences compete with, and may even overshadow, parental influences.

The psychosocial development that occurs during adolescence is largely centered on establishing a personal identity. An important task of adolescence is to learn how to respond appropriately to the development of pubertal sexual characteristics and urges. How this stage of psychological development is accomplished is a crucial factor in determining the attitudes and feelings a person has about sex in adulthood.

Spiritual Influences

Scientists debate whether it is biology or environment that most strongly determines attitudes and behaviors. However, the gospel of Jesus Christ teaches that there is another factor beyond nature and nurture that influences a person's characteristics. Within every man and woman is an individual spirit, possessing agency to make choices that can mold, influence, and even override the input of both genes and environment. This spirit is also sensitive to the influence of the

Holy Ghost, which can give wisdom and strength to choose virtuously between competing impulses.

Every man and woman is a spirit son or daughter of God. The proclamation on the family states that "gender is an essential characteristic of individual premortal, mortal, and eternal identity and purpose." The combination of the spirit and the physical body make up the soul of man (D&C 88:15). Spirits, even when housed in physical bodies, are not inert, nor are they identical. They have individuality, personality, and gender. They respond to light and truth and are quickened by the influence of the Holy Ghost (D&C 93:30–32).

The spirit body, which is the offspring of Heavenly Parents, accounts for many of the individual personality traits that people have. For example, Abraham possessed leadership qualities that he brought with him from his premortal life (Abraham 3:23). His actions reflected his particular spiritual strengths. We know that some of God's most choice spirit children were held back from coming to the earth until this last dispensation because of their valiance and strength in the premortal life (*Ensign,* November 1995:47). Some people have been informed of their spiritual strengths in their patriarchal blessings.

A second powerful spiritual factor that influences people's character and behavior is the Holy Ghost, a gift we receive at baptism and can enjoy continually if we are worthy of it. The Lord's powers are inestimable, as is His ability to change men's hearts if men will let Him. Nephi taught that "the Lord is able to do all things according to his will, for the children of men, if it so be that they exercise faith in him," (1 Nephi 7:12).

On this subject, Elder James E. Talmage wrote, "Subtler, mightier, and more mysterious than any or all of the physical forces of nature are the powers that operate upon conscious organisms, the means by which the mind, the heart, the soul of man may be energized by spiritual forces," (*Discourses,* 14). In other words, spiritual forces are potentially stronger than biological or environmental forces.

Through the refining influence of the Spirit, a man or woman can overcome mortal weaknesses. Their attitudes and behaviors can change. In addition, the Holy Ghost gives people the ability to magnify the godly attributes they were given at birth, even though they may remain in a rudimentary state until activated by the Spirit (*see* Pratt, *Key to Theology,* 101).

DOES THIS MATTER?

Sexual attitudes and behaviors are a by-product of powerful biological, environmental, and spiritual influences. Through an understanding of these things, we can gain insight into how we function and how our spouse functions.

It has been shown that perceived sexual stimuli are processed in male brains differently than in female brains. As a result, "male physiology" leads men to have a higher sex drive and to exhibit more aggressive sexual behavior than women. This tendency is often reinforced by cultural stereotypes, but its precursors are biological. Men don't wake up and consciously decide, "I'm going to be a real he-man today!" Their thoughts and actions are influenced by biological impulses.

Men are also notorious for not being willing or able to talk about their feelings. This problem has its roots in societal norms. Young girls are encouraged to express their feelings, particularly when they are hurt, whereas a boy often grows up being warned to hold his feelings inside and "be a man." As a result of this conditioning and some biological input, women are often more capable than men of communicating emotions. Men are sometimes particularly inept at expressing their feelings on sexual issues.

Knowing these facts, a woman whose husband tends to rush through sex has two choices: she can either resent his insensitivity and accuse him of being thoughtless, or she can try to appreciate the fact that he may simply be exhibiting his biological and cultural tendencies—and then be patient enough to teach him to slow down. He will, if she teaches him with kindness and love. A man whose wife is reluctant to engage in sexual relations also has two choices. He can think she is an uncaring prude, or he can recognize that she may be expressing her own legitimate biological and emotional needs—and then look for ways to help her feel more comfortable with their sexual relationship. And she will, if she knows that he has her best interests at heart.

None of these factors, whether societal or biological, excuses inappropriate behavior. No one is ever justified in saying, "I can't help what I am or what I did." Natural desires can and should be kept in check through self-control. Everyone has agency, the power to determine how to act. That being true, no sane man or woman carries a burden of sexual tendencies or inclinations to which they cannot respond honorably and virtuously.

Fortunately, there is a power that can help men and women understand, harness, and ultimately modify the influences of biology and environment. Everyone is entitled to the blessings of the atonement and the Spirit of the Lord to help them control their actions. The Lord "knoweth the weakness of man and how to succor them," (D&C 62:1). He can change hearts, heal problems, soothe painful memories, remove past sins, and do whatever else is necessary to make things right, if we will let Him into our lives. If there are circumstances that directly or indirectly impact marital intimacy in a negative manner, people can ask the Lord for help, and He will do what He can within the limits of their agency.

DIFFERENCES—GOOD OR BAD?

Many look upon the differences between men and women in a negative light—even as a curse. You hear men say, "I really wish women were more like men," and women say, "wouldn't if be nice if men were more like women." But whether we like it or not, men and women have differences that are deep seated and innate. And every couple has two choices regarding their differences. They can either resent them and forever experience conflict, or they can adapt, accommodate, and find a common ground where they can build their intimate life and enjoy peace and harmony.

One of the secrets of successful marriage is the discovery that differences need not be divisive. They can be the basis of "creative tension" in the relationship: a reason to talk, work together, and compromise. Ultimately, it's nice to be married to someone who is different from us, who can introduce us to alternative opinions, and who has strengths that compensate for our weaknesses. In fact, spouses often lead their partners along exciting paths that they wouldn't normally explore on their own. It is the discovery and blending of contrasting interests and abilities, within a context of mutual cooperation and respect, that allow couples to create wonderful marriages.

CHAPTER 8

Sexual Dysfunction

Janet was a forty-two year-old woman who went to the doctor for her annual exam. She had been in for many previous visits, all of which were unremarkable. In all her times to the office, she had never mentioned any problems. On this occasion, however, when asked if she had any questions, tears came to her eyes. She hesitated, composed herself, and then confided that she had recently lost all interest in being sexually intimate with her husband. This was creating a significant amount of stress in her marriage, particularly because she and her husband had always enjoyed this aspect of their relationship.

She described her husband as a tender partner with whom she was deeply in love. He was equally distraught over her sudden loss of sexual interest. As a part of the evaluation, Janet was asked about the level of stress in her life. Just hearing the question caused her to become tearful again. She stated that she was the mother of three children and had always worked to provide the "extras" in the family. After fifteen years in her current job, her responsibilities had increased dramatically. In her mid-level management role, she was now required to make important decisions on a regular basis. She enjoyed her employment, but had to work long hours. At the end of each day, she was emotionally and physically exhausted, but she still had to face the homemaking responsibilities of cooking, cleaning, and laundry that awaited her.

The oldest child, a daughter, was getting ready to leave for college. Janet felt like she was losing her best friend and the only one in the family inclined to help around the house. Her youngest child, a son in junior high school, was having problems in school and had recently been sent home for smoking. She was greatly concerned about him and couldn't sleep well because of worrying about his problems. As if this wasn't enough, Janet's mother had passed away a year earlier, and the major responsibility of looking after her father had fallen on her shoulders.

It was very distressing to her that she was now having problems in the bedroom, the one place where she had always felt things had gone well in her marriage. To lose her sexual desire now was a tremendous burden.

Janet's physical examination appeared normal. A series of blood tests were in the normal range. There were no obvious medical problems. Ultimately, the doctor determined that Janet's loss of interest in sexual matters was due to the stress of her busy life. During a subsequent visit to the doctor, Janet and her husband, Jerry, were told that her loss of interest was due to situational factors. The doctor reassured them that her interest in sex would most likely return when her life became less busy. Ideas for simplifying her schedule were proposed, and her husband was encouraged to be more patient, understanding, and helpful at home. They seemed comforted by the fact that the problem could probably be cured once a few changes were made in their lives.

Janet and Jerry were encouraged to test the doctor's hypothesis. They arranged a vacation without the children. Upon their return, they happily reported that things had improved. After just a few days together, without the pressures and stresses of day-to-day living, Janet began to feel her normal self again. Since having a fulfilling sex life was a high priority for them, the two committed themselves to make permanent changes in their lives to ensure that Janet's sexual desire would return to where it once was.

SEXUAL DYSFUNCTION DEFINED

Sexual dysfunction is a disturbance in sexual desire or the ability to respond physically in a normal way during sexual relations. It is a common problem for both men and women. Medical studies indicate that thirty to thirty-five percent of men and forty to forty-five percent of women experience sexual dysfunction at some point in their lives. It can be a source of significant unhappiness in marriage, particularly when it continues for a long period of time.

Sexual dysfunction is defined as a problem in any one of the following areas (Laumann, 537):

- A lack of sexual desire
- Arousal difficulties
- The inability to experience orgasm
- Orgasm that occurs too quickly
- Anxiety about sexual performance
- Physical pain during intercourse
- Not finding sex pleasurable

When recent data were analyzed by sex and age group, several patterns emerged. It showed that men and women have different problems, and the nature of these problems changes with age. For example, younger women have more pain associated with intercourse, more anxiety concerning their sexual relations, less ability to achieve orgasm, and less pleasure in their sexual activity than older women, while the latter have more difficulty becoming sexually aroused and lubricated. Older men have more frequent erectile dysfunction and less interest in sex than younger men.

Both psychological and physiological problems can contribute to sexual dysfunction. Studies show that men and women who have emotional and stress-related problems are more likely to experience sexual dysfunction. Also, as men's health deteriorates, they experience more sexual problems than do women.

Problems with sexual function are frequently associated with feelings of unhappiness and low self-esteem in both men and women. This, in turn, contributes to more sexual difficulties. They tend to reinforce each other.

Major marital discord is one of the most common causes of sexual problems. Contention in a relationship diminishes sex drive and one's ability to respond to and enjoy sexual relations. Fortunately, in most cases, these problems reverse themselves if and when marital problems are resolved. However, it is possible for unresolved sexual problems to poison all aspects of the relationship, especially if they continue for long periods of time.

THE TREATMENT OF SEXUAL DYSFUNCTION

Historically, many theories about the causes of sexual dysfunction and their treatment have been postulated. Sigmund Freud was among the first and most famous investigators to attempt to understand problems related to sexual behavior. Most of his theories have fallen into disfavor, but his legacy lives on through continuing research into the sexual problems that afflict so many individuals and couples.

This chapter will describe the most common sexual problems that husbands and wives face, their possible causes, and potential treatments. Fortunately, the vast majority of sexual problems can be treated successfully, thus allowing virtually millions of couples to enjoy their sexual experiences and overcome the embarrassment and frustration created by sexual dysfunction.

TYPES OF SEXUAL DYSFUNCTION

Sexual dysfunction is usually characterized according to the phase of the sexual response in which the problem exists. The phases are desire, excitement, and orgasm. Some people have problems in just one phase, but many have problems in all three phases. The list below describes the most common kinds of problems.

1. Desire Phase Problems

     Women—Low sex drive and aversion to sex

     Men—Low sex drive

2. Excitement Phase Problems

     Women—Inability to become aroused (female sexual arousal disorder)

     Men—Inability to become aroused (impotence or erectile dysfunction)

3. Orgasm Phase Problems

     Women—Inability to experience orgasm (anorgasmia or female orgasmic disorder)

     Men—Male orgasmic disorder (premature ejaculation and retarded ejaculation)

LOW SEX DRIVE

The story of Janet at the beginning of this chapter describes an example of low sex drive. In medical terminology, it is known as

Hypoactive Sexual Desire Disorder (HSDD). The problem afflicts twenty-two to thirty-five percent of women and ten to fifteen percent of men (Kolodny, 564). One researcher stated that HSDD alone was responsible for about forty percent of the referrals for sex therapy in her clinic (*see* Kaplan, *Disorders*).

This category of sexual dysfunction includes not only men and women with a low sex drive, but also those who have absolutely no interest in being sexually intimate with their spouses. A low sex drive may be a lifelong problem, or it may come on gradually over time. However, in defining HSDD, it should be remembered that it is natural for sexual desire to taper off with age; therefore, in some cases "less" may be normal.

The causes of low sex drive are divided into medical and psychosocial causes. Although exact numbers are hard to come by, it is estimated that in the under-fifty age group, ten to twenty percent of low sexual desire is due to medical problems, and eighty to ninety percent is related to psychological problems. These percentages shift in the over-age-fifty group, where low sexual desire is more commonly due to the affects of aging, illness, and medication.

The brain is the center of the human sexual response. The hypothalamus sits deep within the brain and is located in a critical area that is anatomically and functionally at the crossroads of a variety of nervous signals. The hypothalamus and other nearby structures determine the intensity of sexual desire and help determine sexual behavior. They have been dubbed the "sex centers" of the brain. One early researcher hypothesized how the sex centers work. Her relatively simplistic description, given in 1979, is still a fair representation of what is known today:

> The neural organization that governs libido [sexual desire] is similar to that which produces hunger, thirst, and the urge to sleep. Like these other drives, it is served by its own specific network of centers and circuits. The behavioral correlate of neural activity in these centers is the experience of sexual desire. In the absence of such activity there is no libido.
>
> When a patient's sexual drive is constitutionally low, . . . the sex centers are hypoactive on a physiologic basis, [thus]

sexual appetite is low because [sexual signals are] not generated. But in [HSDD] libido is diminished because it is
actively, albeit unconsciously and involuntarily, suppressed
on the basis of psychological conflict. (Kaplan, *Disorders,*
78, 82.)

Put simply, a low sex drive is due either to the absence of sexual
signals within the brain or the suppression of those signals.

When sexual signals are present, they are enhanced or diminished
by a number of internal and external factors. For example, the sex
centers are highly responsive to the hormone testosterone, which
markedly increases the sex drive. They are also influenced by aroma,
sight, sound, touch, a variety of chemicals that cannot be consciously
detected, called pheromones, and memories of previous experiences.
These influences can greatly increase or decrease an individual's sex
drive, depending upon the nature of the stimulus.

In addition, interest in sexual activity is turned off in the brain in
a conscious or unconscious way because of threats that are perceived
by the individual, whether they are real or imaginary. Such threats
include fear, mood shifts, changes in circumstances, changes in relationship dynamics, surgery, illness, fatigue, depression, and situations
that threaten physical harm.

Medical Causes of Low Sex Drive

Medical causes of low sex drive include a variety of health conditions. Hypothyroidism, kidney failure, urologic disease, a variety of
neurologic diseases, tuberculosis, pituitary gland tumors, heart disease,
drug addiction, blood disorders, and adrenal gland problems can all
diminish sexual desire. Any disease that is chronic in nature, such as
liver disease, lung disease, hypertension, and cancer, may have similar
effects. Chronic pain, prolonged immobilization, accidents, damage to
the spinal cord, or surgery that results in disfigurement or a change in
body image may also cause an individual to lose sexual desire.

A variety of medications and drugs can contribute to a low sex
drive. Narcotics, anticancer agents, high blood pressure medications,
antiseizure drugs, antidepressants, alcohol, sedatives, and marijuana
can also inhibit or destroy the sex drive.

Psychological Causes of Low Sex Drive

The vast majority of cases of inhibited sexual desire are the result of psychological, emotional, or social problems, particularly in those under age fifty. These problems may be easily remedied, or so complex that they take years to identify and treat.

Persons who have low sexual desire due to psychological problems typically have little knowledge of what may have created the problem. Sometimes the turn-off mechanisms within the brain began so many years earlier that the person does not remember ever having any sexual desires at all. These individuals frequently refuse to accept that their lack of sexual desire is psychological in origin.

Kaplan divided the psychological causes of low sex drive into mild, mid-level, and deep causes. *Mild causes* of low sexual desire include anger, hostility, performance anxiety, failure to communicate one's needs, repeated unpleasant sexual experiences, partner insensitivity or coercion, power struggles, mistrust, guilt, and memories of strong injunctions against sex. *Mid-level causes* are related to fear: fear of success, pleasure, rejection, losing control, love, and intimacy. *Deep causes* involve serious psychological disturbances, perhaps due to problems in childhood or the remote past. This includes psychological trauma that is not remembered or acknowledged consciously, such as a history of abuse, and other significant emotional insults. Any and all of these problems can diminish or completely destroy sexual desire.

Treatment of Low Sex Drive

Couples can often figure out and treat their own sexual problems through self-education and improved communication. In some cases, however, professional help is necessary to resolve the problems. Most medium to large communities have able counselors who can give advice regarding basic sexual problems. For more difficult cases, a referral to a person trained in the management of sexual dysfunction may be necessary.

In 1970, the first techniques for treating human sexual problems were published. The therapy emphasized education and modification of behavior. Some of the treatment methods developed then are still in use today. A technique called Sensate Focus has been described in literally dozens of texts and self-help books and still forms the cornerstone of treatment of several kinds of sexual dysfunction.

In 1974, another researcher demonstrated that couples with sexual dysfunction improved faster if attention was given to solving the underlying problems in their interpersonal relationship (*see* Kaplan, *New Sex Therapy*). A two-pronged therapy, consisting of behavior modification and marriage counseling, now serves as the basis for most mainstream sexual therapy in the United States today.

When men and women experience sexual problems, the first step in treatment is to identify the point or points in the sexual response where the dysfunction exists. This is how a mechanic approaches automotive repair: correcting the problem depends upon diagnosing the part that is broken. It serves no purpose to replace the carburetor if the starter is dead. So it is with sexual dysfunction.

The next step is to decide if the problem is physiological or psychological in origin. If a medical problem is present, specific treatment is initiated. If the problem is psychological in nature, behavior modification is encouraged, counseling is undertaken, or medication is prescribed.

Treatment often involves helping the individual or couple come to terms with current or past conflicts. People are encouraged to make positive and constructive changes that will enhance their relationship and foster a sense of personal worth. Self-respect is one of the greatest determinants of sexual desire. During treatment of low sexual desire, a husband and wife are often invited to share their "sexual scripts" with each other. This involves an open discussion of a person's wants and desires and sets the stage for constructive compromise and change. Regarding scripts, Carlfred Broderick gave this insight:

> Individuals come into marriage with scripts for marital interaction which may be quite dissimilar. Nowhere is this more likely to happen than in the sexual area. The scripts may be based on parental models, on friends' stories, on books read, on experience with previous partners—on any of a thousand things. As with other scripts, they are taken

for granted and seldom spelled out clearly even in an individual's own mind. (*Couples,* 139.)

In resolving sexual difficulties, the husband and wife are encouraged to state clearly what their desires are and to listen to their spouse's desires. Each partner is encouraged to follow their spouse's scripts, rather than their own, with the understanding that pleasing a spouse "their way" will be more fulfilling than "my way." In the sexual arena, both marriage partners must be willing to make changes since sexual dysfunction is a "couple" problem, not an "individual" problem.

A number of other caveats regarding how to deal with the issue of low sex drive are noteworthy:

- A specific cause for a low sex drive cannot always be isolated. In these cases, dwelling on the past has little value. Individuals must be willing to look forward and make changes in attitude, behavior, and expectations (Kolodny, 520).

- Adherence to outdated societal or cultural stereotypes can be a major hindrance in a relationship. For example, the idea that a man must initiate all sexual activity in marriage can place artificial limitations on sexual intimacy that are counterproductive to the relationship.

- A difference in libido between spouses does not necessarily constitute HSDD on the part of the less interested spouse; it's simply evidence of their different natures. For example, if one partner desires sexual intimacy daily, and the other weekly, this does not constitute HSDD on the part of the less interested spouse.

AVERSION TO SEX

Some people develop another kind of sexual dysfunction called aversion to sex. The medical term for this problem is Sexual Aversion Disorder (SAD). It is a desire phase problem that is much more common among women than men, although it is relatively rare. On the surface, this problem looks like it's an extreme version of HSDD, or low sex drive. In reality, the problem is quite different. Those with a low sex drive may participate in sexual activity with their spouses because they want to be physically intimate or please their spouse, even though they themselves have no desire for sexual relations. Those with an aversion to sex, however, actually feel anger, revulsion, or fear when a potential sexual situation presents itself. Some may actually become physically ill in these settings.

Individuals develop sexual aversion as a result of experiences that are emotionally or physically traumatic. For example, women who have been molested or raped are more likely to develop SAD. Repeated episodes of painful sex can also cause an aversion to sex.

Once again, the treatment of this problem is based upon identifying the cause. If SAD is due to a physical problem, appropriate treatment, aided by personal counseling, may allow an individual to return to normal function. If the aversion to sex is due to past emotional or psychological trauma, intensive psychotherapy is required. Sadly, a complete cure may never be possible for some.

AROUSAL PROBLEMS

The second phase of the sexual response is the excitement phase. Men and women with problems in this phase experience little or no arousal when stimulated physically or sexually. They don't respond to sexual cues from the spouse and they deny feelings of sexual excitement or pleasure.

Women

Excitement phase problems in women are termed female sexual arousal disorder, but historically people have used the more pejorative term "frigidity" to describe the absence of arousal and orgasm in women. One recent report estimates that about fourteen percent of women experience arousal disorders (Laumann, 537).

When a woman doesn't experience arousal, there is an absence of physiologic and anatomic changes of the genital structures. Vasocongestion, or dilation of the blood vessels of the pelvic area, does not occur. Hence, there is no enlargement or lubrication of the vaginal canal, which prepares a woman for penile penetration, and there are no feelings of pleasure associated with sexual activity. This ultimately makes consummation of sexual intercourse difficult and uncomfortable. In addition, without arousal, a woman is incapable of experiencing orgasm.

Men

Excitement phase problems in men are termed impotence or erectile dysfunction. This is a rather common problem. One expert determined that "the prevalence of erectile disorders is forty percent of men at age forty and sixty-six percent at age seventy," (Maurice, *Sexual Medicine*, 255).

Impotence can be present early in life, but typically it is more common after age fifty. Sometimes a weak erection may be present, but then the erection is lost when the couple attempts intercourse. As is the case with women, if complete arousal does not take place, orgasm or ejaculation usually cannot occur.

There are over eighty medical causes of impotence, including a variety of illnesses and medications. Conditions such as abnormal anatomy, acute or chronic disease, surgery, hormonal abnormalities, infections, vascular disease, and neurologic problems may cause impotence. Medications including barbiturates, digoxin, imipramine, phenothiazines, propranolol, and diuretics may contribute to or cause impotence. Alcohol, narcotics, and marijuana can also cause erectile dysfunction.

Over twenty-five psychological causes for impotence have also been identified. The general categories are developmental factors, emotional problems, interpersonal problems, and cognitional factors, such as ignorance or fear (Kolodny, 508–10). Sometimes it is possible to identify a single medical or psychological cause. However, the majority of men with impotence are afflicted by more than one cause.

The treatment of excitement phase problems is generally the same as for low sex drive. Medical problems that might be the cause of the problem are first ruled out. Medications that might cause impotence or lack of arousal need to be evaluated and adjusted. A psychological evaluation, to discover and treat a possible emotional basis for lack of arousal, may also be necessary.

Sensate Focus

Sensate Focus, as mentioned earlier, helps with several kinds of sexual dysfunction. It forms the foundation for treatment of excitement and orgasm phase disorders. The techniques are useful for both men and women who experience a lack of sexual arousal.

When using Sensate Focus therapy, couples are given specific instructions or "homework" assignments that they are to complete in a relaxed setting on a scheduled basis. These assignments require that they participate in intimate physical contact that is initially nonsexual in nature. They then progress to sexual stimulation, sexual intercourse, and orgasm over a designated number of weeks, typically about six.

In the first week or two, Sensate Focus requires that a couple engage in nonsexual touching that is mutually pleasurable. Backrubs, caressing nonsexual areas, and an open discussion of what each enjoys is encouraged, but touching of sexual areas and sexual intercourse are prohibited during the initial part of the program. As the couple successfully accomplishes this first stage, they are allowed to slowly advance to more sexually intimate activities until full intercourse and attempts at orgasm are allowed. Success rates with Sensate Focus vary according to the kind of problem the couple has, but the rates are quite high.

Sensate Focus accomplishes two purposes. The first is for the husband and wife to discover ways of touching each other that are pleasurable and stimulating for the partner. The second is to teach the couple how to provide enjoyment for each other without the expectation that sexual intercourse or orgasm will occur. This helps the husband or wife learn that they can enjoy sexual intimacy without the psychological pressure to proceed to a sexual climax.

Self-Treatment

In most cases where arousal problems have not been lifelong, or where they come and go unpredictably, full-fledged sex therapy and the use of Sensate Focus techniques are not required. The couple can often solve their own problems by discussing the issue, by showing increased tenderness and sensitivity, and resolving any marital conflicts. For example, lack of arousal that occurs sporadically may be due to the fact that a husband and wife are just not on the same wavelength with each other when sexual activity is initiated. They may not be tuned in to each other's desires, needs, and expectations on a particular occasion or over a period of time. Or, it may occur because one partner has been unkind or insensitive, or because there are significant problems in other aspects of the relationship. In other cases, the couple may not be allowing themselves sufficient time to enjoy foreplay with each other. These problems are usually remedied by having positive, honest talks about personal needs and desires or by adjusting the timing and setting of sexual activity.

A man whose wife has difficulty with arousal may need to be more aware of the many demands and pressures that she faces. He may need to be more helpful with family responsibilities so that she can relax emotionally and prepare herself for sexual intimacy. Conversely, the woman whose husband experiences situational impotence must be sensitive to her husband's need for adequate foreplay and the importance of providing sexual cues that he responds to. Unkind words or sarcasm can be very destructive. When a man has difficulty with impotence, he worries that it may occur every time they attempt intercourse, hence the need for constant encouragement and understanding.

ORGASM PROBLEMS

The third phase of the sexual response is orgasm, or sexual climax. Orgasm disorders in women are called anorgasmia or female orgasmic disorder. The most common orgasm disorders in men are premature ejaculation and retarded ejaculation.

Women

The clinical diagnosis of anorgasmia in a woman may seem simple: either she can have an orgasm or she can't. However, in many cases, a woman is unable to determine whether she is having an orgasm. Perhaps she finds sexual intimacy very pleasurable, but doesn't respond in a way that fits the textbook descriptions of orgasm. In this case, she may be having an orgasm without recognizing it, or she may be experiencing sexual fulfillment without orgasm. The question is whether this is a concern for her. No woman has a problem in this area unless she determines there is a problem. Orgasm is not the main or only object of sexual intimacy. If a woman experiences sexual satisfaction and fulfillment with her husband, her ability to achieve orgasm is unimportant. There is no need for her to meet someone else's performance expectations. She may, however, need to find ways to reassure her husband that she enjoys intimacy and that she is fully satisfied with their sexual relationship.

Orgasm requires a high level of sexual arousal for most women. But each body is unique, and every person responds distinctively to varying kinds and levels of stimulation. One method of achieving orgasm is not inherently preferable to all others. In most cases of female anorgasmia, the type or amount of stimulation during foreplay has been inadequate. For example, many women need direct clitoral stimulation to achieve a climax, and without it, orgasm will not occur. Sexual climax usually takes much longer for women to achieve than men. Fifteen to thirty minutes of preparation may be needed.

In addition, female orgasm not only requires the right kind of physical stimulation over a proper time frame, but it also requires the absence of emotional barriers in the relationship. Some women cannot reach orgasm if they fear relinquishing emotional control—if they are concerned that they might be embarrassed or vulnerable if an orgasm occurs. Others need a stress-free environment, without worries about children or whether the doors are locked. Women also need high levels of trust—a feeling that they can expose themselves physically and emotionally without fear of criticism or ridicule.

For women, orgasm is largely a learned experience. It usually doesn't occur with the immediacy and ease of male orgasm. Reaching the orgasm phase in women requires patience, sensitivity, and communication in the relationship so that the couple can learn what works and what does not. Not uncommonly, this is a journey that takes months, or even years, to accomplish.

Men

The most common orgasmic phase problem for men is premature ejaculation. Simply defined, it is the inability to withhold ejaculation until it is desired. Premature ejaculation is present in at least one third of men, although it is higher among men who are newly married. It tends to decrease as the newness of the relationship wears off.

In attempting to define premature ejaculation it must be understood that orgasm is not a totally voluntary event. Once a certain threshold of sexual stimulation is reached, orgasm usually cannot be forestalled. Premature ejaculation occurs essentially because the man reaches this threshold sooner than the couple desires.

Several causes for premature ejaculation have been described. Many experts feel it is a learned behavior from repeatedly rushing through the sexual experience, rather than taking the time to enjoy it. Premature ejaculation can also occur because of an anatomic problem with the veins of the penis, a problem called congenital venous leak. More commonly, premature ejaculation occurs because of the man's anxiety about the sexual experience or marital relationship.

Premature ejaculation is a significant cause of embarrassment, frustration, low self-esteem, and even marital disharmony. Often men discontinue sexual activity altogether rather than deal with the problem. The wife of a man who suffers from premature ejaculation may also experience frustration if her husband's embarrassment results in a hasty end to their intimacy.

A less common form of orgasmic dysfunction in men is retarded ejaculation, or the inability to ejaculate during sexual intercourse. Men may have this problem for the same reasons that women experience anorgasmia. As with impotence, there are a wide variety of organic and psychogenic causes for retarded ejaculation. Again, specific techniques for helping men with this problem have been developed, primarily involving Sensate Focus.

Treatment of Orgasm Problems

The formal treatment of female orgasmic disorder involves the Sensate Focus techniques discussed earlier. When used for anorgasmia, it is particularly important for the Sensate Focus interaction to be "expectation-free." The wife should focus on sensations and feelings and should not be pressured to proceed to intercourse or orgasm any faster than she desires. Often this takes six weeks or more.

Premature ejaculation cannot be treated until the cause of the problem is known. This requires examination by a physician skilled in this area, usually a urologist. If a vascular problem in the penis is discovered, it can be repaired surgically. However, only a relatively small number of cases fit this category.

Again, Sensate Focus is the foundation for the treatment of premature ejaculation. Another treatment, called the "squeeze technique," has been developed to prevent premature ejaculation. With this technique, if the man thinks that he may be approaching ejaculation before he wants to, the wife squeezes the penis near the glans (or tip) in order to delay ejaculation until it is desired. High success rates in the ninety-five to ninety-seven percent range have been reported using these two techniques together.

As with other kinds of sexual dysfunction, if the couple is unable to resolve the problem themselves, they may need to seek counseling to address the underlying causes of the orgasmic dysfunction that may be present.

EDUCATION

In simple terms, whether through self-learning, the help of a spouse, or a counselor's assistance, the treatment of sexual problems consists primarily of education. Elder Hugh B. Brown made reference to this when he advised couples to avoid "gross ignorance" by obtaining "sound instruction" in the subtleties and principles of the normal sexual response (*You and Your Marriage*, 73–74). Couples educate themselves through study, open discussion, and teaching one another. This allows them to break habits and alter behavior patterns that may otherwise keep them from experiencing normal and enriching sexual relations.

The primary purpose of sex therapy is education. It clarifies principles and teaches specific techniques that enhance sexual interaction. It also addresses problems in the relationship, such as communication difficulties, power struggles, and emotional insensitivity. In general, it helps couples understand their marriage relationship and encourages them to better work together.

Sex therapy can be very effective. Depending on the nature and severity of the problem, research shows that formal therapy is successful in curing over seventy percent of the sexual problems that married couples face. Some specific problems, such as premature ejaculation, have a success rate of nearly one hundred percent.

As problems are overcome, sexual intimacy improves. When sexual intimacy is improved, the relationship is enhanced, and a positive cycle is established. In this way, sexual intimacy becomes what the Lord intended it to be—a bond that knits lives together, a source of joy, an expression of love, and an ennobling, enriching influence in the marriage.

Chapter 9

The Early Years

After the honeymoon, a couple usually settles into a pattern of sexual activity that is to their mutual liking. Sexual relations play a different role in each marriage depending upon the needs and desires of the two individuals. For the majority of young couples, the sexual relationship nourishes and strengthens the marriage. However, problems can occur on the honeymoon that continue long after the honeymoon is over. Other problems may develop over time. Over the long haul, uncorrected sexual problems will detract from the quality of the marriage and can even destroy it. This chapter will discuss the transition from the honeymoon to married life as well as addressing the problem of painful intercourse after the honeymoon.

HEATHER AND DEREK

Heather was a young mother who outwardly appeared to be adjusting well to the challenge of caring for two young children. However, she was an intensely private person. Over the course of two pregnancies, she had never revealed much about herself to her doctor. It was surprising, therefore, when she made a doctor's appointment to talk about some problems she was having. She didn't know where else to turn.

Heather indicated that her husband was very angry over her loss of interest in sex. Since the birth of her one-year-old son, her desire for sexual intercourse had vanished, and she could no longer reach an orgasm. Her husband, Derek, was quite upset about it, and she wanted to know what she could do to fix the problem.

The doctor asked Heather to describe her marriage. She disclosed that she and Derek were having serious marital problems. In the four years of their marriage, their relationship had deteriorated to the point that they fought about everything. He preferred spending time with his friends to being with the family. They couldn't agree on whether or not to have any more children. Significant financial problems weighed heavily on them. Derek had stopped going to church, and would instead sit at home watching TV sports. If Heather asked him to do anything, he became defensive or complained that she was nagging.

The doctor asked Heather why she had married Derek, given his demeanor and their disparate views on so many things. She said it hadn't always been this way. They had a wonderful courtship, during which they would stay up late talking for hours. When they couldn't be together, they talked on the phone. They appeared to have everything in common, including spiritual matters. He seemed like the perfect husband-to-be.

When asked at what point things seemed to unravel for them, she exclaimed, "Right after our honeymoon! The day after we got home, he said that I would have to start working at a certain job. He had already arranged it. I was flabbergasted, since we had previously decided that I would take some time to look around for something I liked." That was just the beginning. The pattern of unexpected changes continued. Over time, Derek revealed himself to be a different man than she had come to love prior to their marriage. Slowly, his interest in her and the children seemed to fade, and he found excuses to be gone from home more frequently. Heather was drastically at odds with the man she thought she loved, and she felt emotionally isolated. Of course she had no desire to be sexually intimate with a man she felt so distant from. What could she do to fix the situation?

THE EARLY MARRIED YEARS—BUILDING THE FIRE

One Hollywood star was asked why he was getting divorced for the third time. His reply was straightforward: "marriage is hard."

After the fun and excitement of the honeymoon are over, a couple begins everyday life together. Soon they experience the frustrations associated with being married to someone who is not always on their best behavior. Although they may feel strong emotional ties to each other, day-to-day experiences can create conflict in the relationship. They discover that living with another person can be hard.

Marriage is not a continuation of the honeymoon. There are exciting and wonderful experiences, to be sure, but most of daily living consists of rather routine, even mundane stuff, like taking out the garbage and doing laundry. President Hinckley once quoted Jenkins Lloyd Jones:

> Anyone who imagines that bliss is normal is going to waste a lot of time running around shouting that he's been robbed. Most putts don't drop. Most beef is tough. Most children grow up to be just people. Most successful marriages require a high degree of mutual toleration. Most jobs are more often dull than otherwise. Life is like an old-time rail journey—delays, sidetracks, smoke, dust, cinders, and jolts, interspersed only occasionally by beautiful vistas and thrilling bursts of speed. The trick is to thank the Lord for letting you have the ride. (*Ensign,* November 1984:86.)

In general, if a couple is to succeed in their marriage, and in sexual intimacy in particular, they must establish patterns of healthy interaction early in the marriage. Here are some suggestions:

- Learn to live in harmony with each other, applying Christlike principles to the relationship.
- Discover and deal with differences that exist.
- Sacrifice personal interests for the good of the relationship.
- Discover and deal properly with potentially troublesome issues (i.e., past abuse or low self-esteem).
- Express feelings and ideas clearly and in a nonthreatening manner.
- Listen without becoming defensive.

If a young couple does these things early in their marriage, they will increase their chances for happiness and success in their relationship. If they fail to do these things, problems may go unresolved, emotional distance may be created, and eventually, significant unhappiness can arise.

Painful Sex

Under normal circumstances, sexual intercourse should never be painful. However, some couples return from the honeymoon and find that sexual intercourse continues to be painful for the wife. It may even be painful for the husband. This leads to inhibited sexual desire and other sexual dysfunction.

Estimates are that about ten to twenty percent of women, and three to five percent of men will experience repeated episodes of painful intercourse. This is a condition that requires medical attention. The causes of painful sex are divided into two general categories: psychogenic and organic.

Pain Due to Psychogenic Causes

Tina, a newly-married pregnant woman, went to her doctor for prenatal care. She stated that the pregnancy was going well except for "morning sickness." Her general exam was found to be normal, but during the pelvic examination she experienced significant pain and was unable to complete the examination. Not wanting to make an issue of it, the doctor discontinued the exam, and Tina got dressed.

Afterward, Tina visited with her doctor. "I've never had an exam before. Is it normal for it to hurt that much?" Tina was reassured that a certain amount of discomfort was normal during a pelvic exam, but the doctor also indicated that her pain seemed to be excessive. He then asked her whether he could ask some sensitive questions. She thought about it for a moment, then replied, "yes."

The physician asked Tina whether she experienced pain during sexual intercourse. Apparently relieved at the opportunity to talk about it, she said that intercourse always hurt her, and because of this she avoided it as much as possible. But she admitted that the avoidance of sexual relations had become a source of conflict in her marriage.

She was then asked if she had ever been molested or raped. She was silent for a few moments. Hesitatingly, she responded that when she was fourteen, her cousin, who was a little older than she, had touched her inappropriately. The improper touching occurred on several occasions, but she was spared any further contact with him when he moved away a year later. However, the sexual molestation had left her suspicious of men and their motives.

She was asked what she thought about sex in marriage. She said that she knew it was acceptable to have sexual relations after marriage, and that she really wanted to share this experience with her husband, but whenever her husband approached her sexually, she could feel her stomach cramping up in anticipation. Her honeymoon had been extremely difficult. Although she was able to have intercourse eventually, she found it unpleasant and painful. She concluded, "if it wasn't for the fact that this is the only way to have kids, I could do without it for the rest of my life."

Subsequent visits to the office allowed the obstetrician to get better acquainted with Tina. In time, she consented to another pelvic examination. It revealed normal anatomy, but she experienced uncontrollable vaginal spasms and significant pain during the exam.

Tina was diagnosed with a condition called vaginismus. She was encouraged to address the problem further, but she declined. Several months later she delivered a healthy baby despite a difficult delivery, which was compounded by her resistance to being examined during labor. Unfortunately, she never returned to the office, even for a postpartum visit, presumably because she was embarrassed and unwilling to address the problem.

Psychogenic pain refers to pain that occurs for psychological reasons. Tina had a classical presentation for vaginismus: vaginal pain that is created by involuntary spasms of the muscles surrounding the lower part of the vaginal canal whenever an object is placed in or near the vagina. The spasms are essentially a protective mechanism for a woman who has been conditioned against sexual intercourse. It is an unconscious response. Usually the psychodynamics behind the vaginismus are not understood by the patient. Many of these patients incorrectly assume that sexual intercourse is always supposed to be painful for women.

The causes of vaginismus are many and varied. They include fear of men, a history of sexual abuse, intense guilt about sex, painful memories, and previous failures at consummating sexual intercourse.

In Tina's case, the vaginismus was likely due to having been molested at age fourteen by her cousin. Sadly, it was not a problem she was willing to address at that point in her life.

When vaginismus is not recognized and treated promptly, it results in a destructive self-perpetuating cycle. As the woman experiences repeated painful sexual relations, which may be compounded by an unknowing or insensitive spouse, her conditioning against physical intimacy is reinforced. Characteristically, these women avoid routine exams and pap smears because vaginismus also occurs in these settings.

Treatment for vaginismus is very successful, however. It involves the use of Sensate Focus techniques, followed by the use of vaginal dilators of gradually increasing size. Patients who use these techniques report virtually one hundred percent success in curing this problem.

Lack of Arousal

Painful intercourse also occurs in women who are unable to become sexually aroused. When there is no arousal, they fail to produce the proper vaginal lubrication, making sexual intercourse difficult or painful. In some cases, it is due to a husband who hurries through the sexual act without being sensitive to his wife's needs and without giving her time to adequately prepare for the experience.

Commercial lubricants are readily available to compensate for this problem. Simple hand or body lotions also work for many couples, but care should be taken since these may cause irritation in some women. If problems appear chronic, appropriate counseling may also be needed.

Pain Due to Organic Causes

Sandy went to her doctor to find out why she couldn't get pregnant. She was thirty-five years old and had been married for eight years. She had been on birth control pills during the first six years of her marriage, but she had not used any contraception for the past two years. When she stopped using birth control pills, she noticed that sexual intercourse began to be painful. Sex now hurt her about half the time. Her menstrual periods also became far more painful after she stopped taking the pills.

Her visit to the doctor did not reveal an obvious cause for her infertility, but she did have moderate pain during her pelvic examination. Laparoscopic surgery was undertaken to further assess the situation. The surgery showed that she had a condition called endometriosis. Surgical removal of the endometriosis, followed by six months of medical treatment, resulted in resolution of her pain. She soon became pregnant and later delivered a healthy baby.

Endometriosis is a relatively common cause of pelvic pain that affects about five percent of women. It is caused by the presence of abnormal tissue on the ovaries, fallopian tubes, or on the outside of the uterus. It causes severe pain during intercourse or menstruation and may also cause infertility. The possible causes of endometriosis have not yet been definitively determined.

Although endometriosis may be suspected on clinical grounds, it can only be diagnosed with certainty through surgical evaluation, usually by laparoscopy. It is more common among women who delay childbearing until later in life, although exceptions occur.

Endometriosis can be treated with surgery or medication. Surgery removes the disease and scar tissue from around the internal genital structures. Medications cause the endometriosis to stop its growth. Recently, new medications called GnRH agonists have proven valuable in treating endometriosis.

The word "organic" is used to describe situations where the pain of intercourse is due to a medical problem. This may involve abnormal anatomy or pathologic processes, such as endometriosis or infection. Pain during intercourse can occur in the external or internal genitalia and can occur in both men and women. The organic causes of painful intercourse are listed below (Kolodny, 183–227).

Organic Causes of Painful Sexual Intercourse in Women

- External genitalia (at or outside the vaginal opening)—intact hymen, inflammation or infection, episiotomy or childbirth scars, skin conditions (including atrophy, dystrophy, and allergic reactions).
- Vagina—infections, foreign objects (i.e., retained tampon), atrophy from lack of estrogen, effects from radiation, inadequate lubrication.

- Uterus—abnormal uterine position (sharply "tipped" or prolapsed), fibroid tumors, uterine infection, endometriosis.
- Fallopian tubes and ovaries—adhesions (scar tissue), tubal infection, tubal pregnancy, endometriosis, ovarian cyst, ovarian tumor, ovulation.
- Other—inflammatory bowel disease, bladder infections, urethral infections or inflammation, low back pain, arthritis, muscle spasms.

Organic Causes of Painful Sexual Intercourse in Men

- External genitalia—penile fibrosis, penile cancer, urethritis, genital herpes, allergic reactions, infections, sickle cell disease, trauma, inflamation of the testes, testicular tumors.
- Internal genitalia—cremasteric muscle spasms, prostatitis, infection of the seminal vesicles.
- Bladder infections, muscle spasms, arthritis, low back pain, hernia with spermatic cord torsion.

Treatment of organic causes of painful intercourse requires identification of the source of the problem. A doctor will usually need to take a careful history, perform a complete examination, and order appropriate laboratory tests, including possible X-rays and ultrasounds. In women, surgery is often recommended to diagnose problems inside the abdomen.

If a husband or wife finds that sexual intercourse is painful, a doctor should be consulted to determine the cause and to treat it appropriately. Women should usually see a gynecologist and men a urologist. However, family physicians can screen for and treat simple problems in both men and women.

SEXUAL INTIMACY DURING PREGNANCY AND POST-PARTUM

Most couples eventually face the issue of what to do about sex during pregnancy. Years ago, doctors routinely prohibited sexual intercourse for the entire pregnancy because of concern that it could cause miscarriage, infection, and preterm birth. It is now known that under normal circumstances, there is no reason to limit sexual activity, including orgasm, during pregnancy. A couple may participate in sexual intercourse throughout pregnancy without undue concern unless the following conditions or problems exist: recurrent miscarriages, incompetent cervix, placenta previa, placenta abruptio, a history of premature labor or delivery, premature labor in the current pregnancy, premature spontaneous rupture of membranes, twin or triplet pregnancy, or a history of bleeding following intercourse. A physician may permit exceptions in some cases.

Although sexual intercourse during pregnancy is usually permissible, not every woman is interested. One wife explained:

> *Having a baby throws an entirely new twist into sexual relations just when you think you have it all figured out. When I was pregnant, I was extremely ill for the first five months. Much to my husband's dismay, any intimate touch made me very sick and often caused me to vomit. Then, when I could finally be intimate without being sick, I was big and it was difficult to find a comfortable position. Well, we survived, but the real trial came after the baby arrived. During my delivery I received an episiotomy, and then I continued to tear. When I went to my OB/GYN for my six-week visit he told me that I could have sex again, but I really had a difficult time for several months after our baby's birth. It got to be a real problem. I started being resentful of my husband, and sex became a very unpleasant thing to me. It has since gotten better, but there are some things I wish my husband and I had known before the pregnancy.*

Men should be sensitive to the fact that during pregnancy and in the post-partum period a woman may not be as interested in being as sexually active as she was before. This can be due to fatigue, physical discomfort, stress, pain, and, in the case of the post-partum period, a lack of hormone production by the ovaries. Intercourse may also be uncomfortable during and after pregnancy. Extra patience and understanding of the woman's physical and emotional state are needed during this time. These problems usually resolve themselves unless there are underlying long-term emotional or physical problems.

Frequency of Sexual Relations

Despite the long list of potential problems a young couple may encounter in their sexual relationship, most actually do pretty well. They are not troubled by significant sexual dysfunction, pain, or emotional barriers to fulfilling sex. If they are, they hope things will work out over time and are willing to be patient. However, most couples do have to deal with one major issue: differing expectations regarding how often to have intercourse. This is the biggest sexual concern confronting those in the early married years.

What is the right amount of sex? There is no "right" amount. What is "right" for one couple is not necessarily "right" for another, and what is desired by one person in the marriage may not be desired by the other. In virtually all relationships, accommodations must be made. Little will be gained by arguing over the fact that the "average" couple has sex a certain number of times per week.

Occasionally, differences in sexual desire are an issue from the first day of the marriage. More commonly, however, differences in sex drive don't appear until after the honeymoon, when there is a significant life event, such as the birth of a baby, an illness, or a new or demanding job. If not handled carefully, arguments and hurt feelings can arise over this issue. This again brings up the need for frequent communication, empathy, and patience in the relationship. It also underscores the fact that marriage is a constantly changing state. Attitudes and behaviors must be re-examined frequently to compensate for the various changes that occur throughout married life.

CHAPTER 10

The Middle Years

As a marriage moves from the "early" to the "middle" years, the dynamics of the relationship often shift. The first few years of marriage are generally concerned with learning to adapt to each other during a time when there aren't too many competing interests, such as children. In contrast, the middle years are largely occupied with learning to deal with careers, changes in financial status, the responsibilities of assuming larger roles in church and society, and the increasing demands of children.

During the middle years, as a couple adapts to the increased demands on their time, resources, and energy, their sexual relationship often changes as well. Consequently, the sexual problems couples encounter in these years are usually different from those experienced earlier in marriage. In addition, pre-existing problems that have not been resolved are amplified during this period when the couple has less time to devote to each other. The following scenario describes one couple's journey from early marriage through the challenging middle years and some of the pitfalls they encountered.

MATTHEW AND SAMANTHA

Matthew and Samantha met during college registration in the fall. Matt was a recently returned missionary, and Sam had just arrived in town to go to college. For several months, there wasn't anything special between them; they were just friends in the singles' ward. However, when they were called to work together in a church assignment, they really hit it off. They discovered many areas of common interest and felt a sense of comfort in each other's presence; they could just be themselves without any pretense. Most importantly, they found they were both committed to spiritual growth and each possessed a love of the gospel.

Soon Matthew and Samantha were spending as much time together as possible. They reveled in their shared emotional and spiritual perspectives. In time, they came to feel that this was a very special relationship and that they should marry. After feeling divine confirmation, they did so.

Matt and Sam found enormous happiness in their marriage. When they weren't at school or work, they spent every moment together. They couldn't imagine a more joyful existence. However, despite their obvious happiness, the early-married years were not without challenges. Matthew was a meticulous individual who felt that everything should have its place and be in it. Sam had a more "free-spirited" approach. If the dishes didn't get done or the laundry folded until later, it didn't matter much. When Matthew mentioned uncompleted housework, she became defensive or tearful, so he sidestepped the issue as much as possible.

In addition, Matthew liked to be in control of the finances. He paid the bills and kept close track of their financial situation. He constantly worried that their limited income would not stretch far enough to meet their needs. Sam, however, had come from a well-to-do family. She did not share Matthew's concern about financial details and even bristled under his overly controlling style. Occasionally, Sam's mother would slip her some money, which bothered Matthew even more. In his mind, that just encouraged Sam's poor spending habits.

After five years of marriage, Matt and Sam were the parents of two children. Sam was completely absorbed in the process of child-raising and loved it. She devoted her entire life to providing for her children's many needs and discovered great joy in the process. Meanwhile, Matthew had graduated from college and was putting in long hours as a junior executive in a growing software company, which he greatly enjoyed.

Eventually, Matthew and Samantha found they were spending very few hours together. After work, Matt usually watched TV in order to wind down. Sam spent her evenings reading or tending to the children. Gradually, it seemed they had less and less time for each other at the end of the day. When they did have a minute together, they were usually very tired. Their discussions were almost exclusively limited to dealing with only the most pressing issues, and the long, intimate conversations they had enjoyed before marriage no longer took place.

After ten years of marriage and the birth of four children, Matt and Sam's lives had become chaotic. Although they were still devoted to each other, much of the luster of the early years had faded, and their marriage now faced significant problems. Sam had run up thousands of dollars of charge-card bills. It was all they could do each month to just pay off the interest. Matthew was disgusted with Sam's lack of responsibility in financial matters and her poor house-keeping skills and frequently mentioned it. He felt as if he were talking to a blank wall since nothing ever seemed to change for the better.

On the other hand, Samantha became less and less tolerant of Matthew's controlling attitude and his long hours away from home. A disproportionate amount of the housework and day-to-day child rearing duties fell on her shoulders. She wondered why he couldn't pitch in and help more when he got home from work. If he cared so much about how things looked around the house, why didn't he help out?

Meanwhile, the children's needs were rapidly expanding. Music lessons, athletic events, scout activities, school functions, and a myriad of other obligations consumed their lives. Matthew and Sam found even less time to talk. Most of their discussions were limited to dealing with children and schedules. They no longer risked sharing their innermost feelings. Indeed, much of their dialogue was in the form of argument. A great gulf was developing between them.

In the fifteenth year of marriage, the widening divide between Matthew and Samantha brought the marriage to the breaking point. While they seemed a model family to friends and neighbors in the ward, they knew their marriage was in trouble. Angry and hurt feelings percolated under the surface of an outwardly normal marriage.

Their uneasy coexistence was laced with private bitterness and the pain of thousands of unkind words. Their physical intimacy had broken down years earlier.

MARITAL MELTDOWN

Many couples, of course, navigate the middle years of marriage without too much difficulty. But Matthew and Samantha's story describes an all-too-common scenario among married couples. It tells of the total collapse that some married relationships experience after many years together. John Gottman refers to it as "marital meltdown."

There are many causes of marital meltdown, but all of them seem to relate to one basic factor: neglect of the marriage. A marriage is a living, dynamic relationship that takes on a life of its own. It must be fed. In order for marriages to be successful, and for the sexual aspect of the relationship to remain a fulfilling part of the marriage, a couple must be able to adapt and change to the problems and stresses that arise. This requires time and attention. When time and attention are withheld, the marriage suffers, and so does sexual intimacy.

Compared to early and later marriage, the middle years of marriage are the most demanding, at least emotionally. During these years, spouses seem to have less time and energy to devote to each other. They are pulled in many directions in their quest to be good parents, employees, church members, and citizens. Meaningful moments alone as spouses can become difficult to find. Consequently, spouses may begin to ignore each other as they give attention to other demands. There is usually a decrease in the frequency of intimate relations and a loss of emotional intensity associated with sexual interaction. For some, sex becomes routine and unfulfilling. For others, it may even be seen as a duty or chore.

Spouses in the second and third decades of marriage may feel as if they are more like business partners than lovers. However, when the couple's intimate life is put on the back burner for too long, one or both spouses can become unhappy and dissatisfied. Over time, if not corrected, the couple may completely stop being physically intimate. Cutting themselves off from the nurturing aspects of sexual intimacy may further stress an already fragile relationship. Thoughts of separation or even divorce may be raised as "greener pastures" become appealing.

SEXUAL DYSFUNCTION IN THE MIDDLE YEARS

Men and women sometimes experience sexual problems in the middle years of marriage even though the early married years were problem-free. Virtually all of the types of sexual dysfunction discussed earlier can occur; however, some problems are more common than others. The most frequent sexual complaint among men and women between thirty and fifty is a loss or reduction of sexual desire. This is generally a more common problem for women, but it is not unusual among men.

The second most common problem for men and women during these years is decreased ability to achieve orgasm. Again, this is more common among women than men, but men are not spared. Men commonly begin having problems with erectile dysfunction in these years. Estimates are that forty percent of men at age forty experience impotence.

In these years, the loss of sex drive and the inability to achieve orgasm are psychological in origin about eighty percent of the time. When significant stress persists, or when the relationship is not going perfectly, the sex drive drops off and the ability to achieve orgasm is diminished.

Conversely, sexual dysfunction in the middle married years is due to physical problems approximately twenty percent of the time. Women may suffer from chronic lack of sleep, fatigue, anemia, thyroid disease, obesity, hormonal problems, and the wear and tear of pregnancy and childbearing. Men may suffer insomnia, fatigue, and the onset of a variety of medical problems such as obesity and hypertension. These medical conditions can have a dramatic impact on sexual desire and the ability to respond normally during sexual intercourse.

IDENTITY CRISIS

Several decades ago sociologists began describing something they called a "mid-life crisis." The phrase was used to describe men who demonstrated dramatic personality and behavior changes in response to feelings of failure or inadequacy as they approached retirement.

This often occurred despite many years of marital stability. However, identity crises are not limited to middle-aged men. This phenomenon is experienced commonly by men and women in their forties and fifties. Witness the number of marriages that end in divorce after fifteen or twenty years because a man or woman has "tired" of the relationship.

Elder David B. Haight lamented:

> Middle-age divorce is particularly distressing as it indicates that mature people, who are the backbone of our society, are not working carefully enough to preserve their marriages. Divorces granted to people over forty-five have increased at an alarming rate. When middle-aged people even consider breaking up their marriage—a couple who may have reared their children, who possibly have grandchildren—and now decide to go their separate ways, they need to realize that every divorce is the result of selfishness on the part of one or both. (*Ensign,* May 1984:13–14.)

Such selfishness erodes the relationship, putting personal concerns above the needs of the marriage and family.

The Middle Married Years—Tending the Glowing Embers

A marriage could be compared to a campfire. The early married years are usually accompanied by intense emotions, typified by a bright flame. In time, the flames of the early years turn to embers that, although less bright, are actually much hotter and more useful. The passion of the early years eventually yields to a more stable relationship with more color and depth. However, a couple cannot neglect the embers. They must add fuel on a periodic basis. If they continue to nurture their relationship, the embers will burn with great intensity. But if the fire is not maintained, even once brilliant embers will die out.

All too often, the embers of a mature relationship are allowed to cool. Couples are lulled into thinking that they don't have to give the marriage the attention they once did. But mature relationships need tender care just as much as young relationships do. The fire must be fed continually.

It is helpful to know how to tend the marriage embers during this phase of the relationship. The following tasks should be addressed during the middle married years to keep marriages strong.

- Adapt to the stress that family life, and specifically children, present to the marriage.
- Deal with the challenges of careers and increasing financial demands.
- Fit into a changing social structure and assume more responsibility in society.
- Overcome any destructive behavior patterns or bad habits that have been established in the early married years.
- Avoid the temptation to put the needs or interests of other people or other things ahead of the needs of the relationship.
- Develop the flexibility to adjust to the changing landscape of family life, including events that arise unpredictably.

Speaking of keeping the marital flame alive, President Harold B. Lee stated:

> Those who allow the marriage ceremony to terminate the days of "courtship" are making a well-nigh fatal mistake. If the new bride were to discover that her husband was just an actor before their marriage and now his quest is ended, he stands revealed as a cheap counterfeit of his former self either in appearance or conduct, that would indeed be a shocking experience. Evidences and tokens of your love and daily proof of your unselfishness toward her and your family will make love's flame burn more brightly with the years. Do you girls suppose that the same attention to personal details is less important after marriage? Surely the same qualities and traits in you that first attracted him are just as important in married life in keeping alive the flame of his affection and romantic desire. (Lee, *Teachings,* 241-42.)

Many of us learn that the more we interact with our spouse and our growing and adult children, the more enjoyable and satisfying life becomes. But, as a check on your own marriage, or to add a little fuel to the fire, stir up the embers, or just to remind yourself of some basic keys of a stable marriage, here are ten things that happily married couples have in common.

    1. **Let the Spirit be present in your marriage relationship.**

Love is one of the fruits of the Spirit, and marital love is its choicest delight. When we live by the standards of the gospel and seek personal inspiration to be a better spouse and parent, we are much more likely to treat each other in Christlike ways. It is impossible for a couple to have the Spirit of the Lord with them and be angry and contentious at the same time. The Savior was clear about this: "I say unto you, he that hath the spirit of contention is not of me, but is of the devil, who is the father of contention," he told the Nephites. "This is not my doctrine, to stir up the hearts of men with anger, one against another; but this is my doctrine, that such things should be done away," (3 Nephi 11:29–30). If you are arguing and contending, you know that you do not have the Spirit of the Lord with you. The solution is to apologize, repent, and bring your relationship back into harmony with eternal principles.

Prophets have been adamant about how husbands and wives should treat each other. President Ezra Taft Benson said, "A priesthood holder who would curse his wife, abuse her with words or actions, or do the same to one of his own children, is guilty of grievous sin. 'Can ye be angry, and not sin?' asked the Apostle Paul (JST, Ephesians 4:26). If a man [or woman] does not control his temper, it is a sad admission that he is not in control of his thoughts. He then becomes a victim of his own passions and emotions, which lead him to actions that are totally unfit for civilized behavior, let alone behavior for a priesthood holder," (*Ensign,* November 1986:47). President David O. McKay, on a similar theme, said, "A man [or woman] who cannot control his temper is not very likely to control his passion, and no matter what his pretensions in religion, he moves in daily life very close to the animal plane," (*Improvement Era,* June 1958:407). President Howard W. Hunter reminded us of President George Albert Smith's conference statement: "We should not lose our tempers and abuse one another. . . . Nobody ever abused anybody else when he had the spirit of the Lord. It is always when we have some other spirit," (in *CR,* October 1950, 8. *See also CR,* October 1994, 69).

Marriage partners who lose the Spirit of the Lord have become careless in living gospel principles, for the promise is extended to them that if they will honor the principles and covenants of marriage, they will find that marriage grows more soul-binding over time. President Harold B. Lee made this promise:

> Those who go to the marriage altar with love in their hearts, we might say to them in truth, if they will be true to the covenants that they take in the temple, fifty years after their marriage they can say to each another; "We must have not known what true love was when we were married, because we think so much more of each other today!"
>
> And so it will be if they will follow the counsel of their leaders and obey the holy, sacred instructions given in the temple ceremony; they will grow more perfectly in love even to a fulness of love in the presence of the Lord Himself. (Lee, *Teachings*, 243.)

Perhaps, for some couples who are struggling, the problem is that the mutual sacrifice and service so evident early in the marriage has ceased; or the spirit they felt in the temple on their wedding day has evaporated due to apathy. Tensions may have escalated over monetary matters, disciplining children, household duties and leadership, decision making, family schedules, work issues, and health matters. However, none of these issues can be allowed to become excuses for abusive behavior. Many couples have resolved these issues in their marriage and have not let the crisis destroy them. Together, they pitched in to overcome them. You cannot afford to do otherwise.

The importance of praying together is probably the most consistent counsel given to couples at the time they marry in the temple. Yet, when contention develops in a marriage, spouses blame each other for perceived faults and failings in the companion, and such accusations cause a loss of the spirit of love and harmony. Anger and bitterness replace good feelings and weaken the marriage commitment. It is hard to kneel in prayer with a companion who is angry, grumpy, critical, mean, or cantankerous. Daily prayer between husband and wife is typically the first casualty of contention.

Couples struggling in marriage also tend to decrease their physical contact. Hugs become less frequent. Good-bye and homecoming kisses are avoided and sexual intimacy drops off substantially, if not completely. The thrill of being together in a physical relationship that was cherished in the earlier years now yields to a demanding schedule of family activities.

There may be several reasons why physical intimacy drops off. A husband's exercise schedule gets neglected because his ankles or knees hurt, and he starts to develop a paunch. After several pregnancies a wife finds it increasingly difficult to take the weight back off. Both may be feeling awkward and insecure about their physical appearance. Finances may be tight. Perhaps the kids are struggling. Stresses from all sides can cause tempers to flare and contention to increase. Sometimes worldly success can lead to pride and criticism of others. If unchecked, negative behaviors and personality traits may emerge, leading to sarcasm, impatience, selfishness, and resentment.

Who would want to share their very soul with such a person? When couples allow pressures and worries to drive them apart, sexual relations can easily be reduced to selfish gratification. In such a situation, true intimacy between a husband and wife is lost, and the joy of their union is defiled. The irony is that these same pressures lead many couples to rely more fully on each other, to fast and pray together, and to find the solace and support that comes through the physical sharing of their souls.

2. Repent of your marital and personality mistakes.

The Lord instructed Joseph Smith to "say nothing but repentance to this generation," (D&C 6:9). The Book of Mormon contains many examples of those who lost their blessings because they would not humble themselves and repent. They became too self sufficient. Their lives were filled with ease and prosperity and they forgot the source of their blessings (Helaman 3:36; 4:11–12; 6:1–6). We learn from that ancient record that whenever the Nephites had unprecedented freedom, economic prosperity, leisure time, and trinkets to buy, they had difficulty keeping their priorities straight. Many of these same conditions exist today, and some are making the same mistakes.

Avoid selfishness. Look at why you do what you do. It is tragic when individuals allow trivial things to make them bitter and angry.

Analyze what part of the marriage or family problem is your responsibility, and then do something to correct it. No doubt there are areas where you can make some positive changes in the relationship. Correct your own weaknesses first, before you start on your spouse. As Carlfred Broderick indicated, we are quick to spot weaknesses:

> After weeks, or even months and years of frustration, the conclusion most people come to is that the problem lies in the character deficiencies of their spouses. If only their partners weren't so lazy or selfish or uncaring or stupid or immature or oversexed or frigid or under the evil influence of their mothers . . . then perhaps there might be hope. Others come to the less popular but still common conclusion that the deficiencies lie in themselves—that they are the ones who are unforgivably crazy, unattractive or dumb. (Broderick, 16.)

So often in a counseling setting, a breakthrough is possible only when one of the spouses will let go of pride and blame to ask forgiveness, saying something like this: "Sweetheart, I know that you are not happy with the way things have been going lately, and I'm not either. But we did have a good thing going when we married. I think we have both gotten careless in the way we treat each other. I want you to know that I'm sorry about my part in this whole thing. I can do better, and I'm going to. I appreciate all you do for me, but I've been ungrateful. Please forgive me. From now on, you can count on me to do my part better." Couples could save a great deal in counseling fees if they would humble themselves and repent—by doing things better or stopping those things that are hurting the relationship. When one spouse makes an effort to improve, the "law of reciprocity" almost forces the other one to make positive changes.

3. **Forgive your spouse's mistakes.**

Wipe the slate clean. If you chew on old offenses, you close yourself off from being charitable and from the chance to make changes in yourself. Evaluate and correct your own imperfections first. Don't keep score. Stop nurturing grudges. Leave the past in the past. Since you can't change the past, work to change yourself in the present, because you can change. That is the good news of the gospel. You have the ability to choose differently than you have in the past. Pick up your life and get over past hurts. We all make mistakes. You make them too, and yours are just as serious, usually, as those of your spouse. Stop trying to remake your companion into a copy of yourself.

4. Enrich your relationship.

Remember when you fell in love. How did it happen? You probably talked a lot together. Try it again, only listen and learn as if it's the first time; and don't interrupt. Remind yourself of the unique person you married and how much fun you had in getting together. Stop correcting your spouse. Read each other's patriarchal blessing. You may have forgotten what a wonderful son or daughter of God you married. It is your responsibility to lift your companion to a higher plane, not pull him or her down. You lift one another by being positive with each other. Use language that blesses, language that you use with clients, patients, customers, church leaders, or neighbors. Schedule regular time together away from the children. You can't expect to retain feelings of love when you neglect your companionship.

President Harold B. Lee wisely taught husbands to monitor their marriage relationship:

> What is our relationship with our wife? Someone has said the opposite of love is not hate; the opposite of love is apathy. And I say to you brethren, the most dangerous thing that can happen between you and your wife or between me and my wife is apathy—not hate, but for them to feel that we are not interested in their affairs, that we are not expressing our love and showing our affection in countless ways. Women, to be happy, have to be loved and so do men. Someone has said that little children soon outgrow their love or their need for the love of a mother, but husbands never do. We need that, but we have to give love; we have to express love to our wives if we expect it in return. (Lee, *Teachings*, 241.)

5. Be humble.

We all need a good dose of humility. Many people, in the relative prosperity of our times, are losing their moorings amid the attractive distractions that bombard us from all sides. The fruits of ease are beginning to show up in our cultural malaise and in our private behavior. A focus on fashions, the lure of leisure, an increased intensity of violence in entertainment and music, a popular indulgence in excessive food and drink, the time-taking temptations of television, labor-saving devices that allow us to spend more time on less valuable pursuits—all of these take their toll on our willingness to work for what is worthy, and we adopt ideas and behaviors that are inconsistent with gospel standards. We can become so busy with these external stimulants that we lose sight of more pressing responsibilities. We would do well to periodically read President Ezra Taft Benson's talk on pride.

6. Participate in activities as a couple.

Increase the amount of positive time you spend together. Take a class. Go for walks. Date more. Get away from the phone and children. Weekend getaways and vacations for the two of you are among the best of all therapies. A cruise can do wonders for a marriage. The bottom line is that babysitters are much cheaper than marriage counselors. A stroll through the park arm in arm or holding hands and renewing your association will add some pizazz to your relationship.

7. Take time—and make time—for physical intimacy.

Nothing perks up a marriage more than being consistent in your physical intimacy. Here is a suggestion to try for two months. Decide on two nights each week to set aside for physical intimacy. Let the husband be responsible for setting the mood and tone on one night while the wife takes care of the other. On their chosen day, the wife or husband arranges the details of the ambience, the place and time, and initiates appropriate sexual activity according to their own script—perhaps with a romantic conversation or a soothing massage. The other spouse agrees to be a willing companion, adventuresome enough to go along with the script. For two days out of the week, you may treat each other even better than you did when you were first married. Then, let your thoughtfulness and cooperation spread to the rest of the week.

8. Develop Christlike personality traits.

You can be no better spouse or parent than you are a person. If you struggle with self-worth and are critical of others, not only will your life be filled with unhappiness, but your children will likely learn from your behavior. Anger is the great destroyer of marriages and families. Improve yourself before you change the world. Take a good look in the mirror. Is your stomach sticking out over your belt? Do you need a new hair-do? What was the last book you read? Decide what you need. Get some exercise. Be cheerful. Learn about computers and E-mail. Say something nice to your spouse without expecting something in return. Eliminate aspects of your personality that are irritating to you and others.

9. Be realistic.

Your spouse carries a heavy load. He or she is already stretched emotionally with many responsibilities. So are you. Don't let work or other concerns interfere with more important things. Find ways to spend more time with your family. Don't take your health and prosperity for granted. Set a little money aside for dates and vacations. Look for ways to ease your spouse's burdens.

10. If you need help, get it.

Consult with a church leader, a trusted friend, a family member, or an outside counselor. Choose a professional wisely. Be sure they have a good record of helping others. Start with the bishop. If he feels you need more help, he will refer you. Harold B. Lee counseled:

> Teach those who are having marriage problems to go to the father of the ward, their bishop, for counsel. No psychiatrist in the world, no marriage counselor, can give to those who are faithful members of the Church the counsel from one any better than the bishop of the ward. Now, you bishops don't hesitate to say, marriage is the law of God, and is ordained by him, and man and wife are not without each other in the Lord. (Lee, *Teachings*, 250–51.)

If you go to a counselor other than the bishop, go together. Counseling just one spouse about marriage and family problems is of little value. There is nothing more frustrating for a counselor or a spouse than to face problem-solving efforts with only one of the parties present. In marriage, if either one of you has a problem, you both do, and both need to contribute to the solution.

A FINAL NOTE

There will be occasional challenges and disappointments for all couples during the middle years of marriage. Fortunately, the majority of Latter-day Saint husbands and wives do quite well during this phase of their lives. This can be a time of fulfillment for both companions.

Marital intimacy should be an important and frequent element of marriage despite the inevitable challenges that arise in every relationship. Intimate exchanges should not be something a couple recalls from the early years of marriage, but should continue to be satisfying for both over a lifetime. Generally, the children are grown or growing up, income is finally adequate, you own a home with rising equity, your companionship is maturing, you are more united in parenting practices, and spiritual experiences confirm again and again the validity of the gospel. These can and should be wonderful years for physical intimacy as well.

CHAPTER 11

The Later Years

When a husband and wife reach their fifties, they pass from what we have called the "middle years" into the "later years" of marriage. Many couples spend more time together in this stage of marriage than any other, since more people are living into their eighties or longer. The sexual problems encountered in this phase of married life are usually due to aging and its affects upon the body. Aging can worsen existing problems and create new ones.

Most sexual problems prior to age fifty are psychological in origin. However, after age fifty, at least one-half of all sexual dysfunction is due to age-related physiologic changes, medical problems, or the use of certain medications. But aging does not have the same effect upon men and women. For example, after age fifty, the incidence of sexual problems gradually increases for men, with impotence and lack of sexual desire becoming the two most common complaints. In contrast, women seem to have fewer sexual problems during these years, because they are now comfortable in their married relationships and are more sure about themselves. In addition, although a woman may have a medical condition that would limit sexual ability for a man, such a condition may not prevent her from being a receptive sexual partner. Therefore, she is less likely to be the one who limits sexual activity because of an inability to perform. Many women also find that they are able to relax and enjoy intimacy more in these later years since they no longer need to worry about the timing or pressures of pregnancy.

The fact that men experience more problems with sexual function after age fifty creates special challenges for many married couples. It often leads to less frequent sexual relations and, unfortunately, some couples become celibate altogether because of male sexual dysfunction. Surveys show that about one-fourth of couples where the husband is over age sixty-six no longer have sexual intercourse (Rinehart and Schiff, 77). Women frequently express frustration over marriages made "sexless" because of their husband's problems.

The woman's relative greater desire for sexual intimacy at this time of life may create a situation that is the opposite of conditions earlier in the marriage. This change in roles in the later years can alter the dynamics of the relationship. The man may be more on the defensive or feel his leadership role is jeopardized. Anger and hurt feelings can also arise, thus detracting from what otherwise would be a wonderful and compatible marriage.

HORMONES

After age fifty, men and women increasingly have sexual problems that are due to hormonal changes. The specific hormone that is most critical to men's sexual function is testosterone. For women, the most important hormone is estrogen, although testosterone also plays an important role in female sexual function.

At about age fifty, men experience a slow and gradual drop in testosterone levels. This decrease in the production of androgens, specifically testosterone, by the testes is sometimes called andropause. It is usually gradual and takes place over several decades. Conversely, at about age fifty, women experience an obvious and more sudden change in hormones that results in menopause. This is caused by a loss of estrogen production by the ovaries.

Men—Andropause

There are significant physical and psychological side effects related to andropause. A loss of testosterone results in a decrease in sexual desire and in an increase in erectile dysfunction. Some men lose all feelings of sexual desire and/or their ability to consummate sexual relations. In addition, fertility decreases as the number and quality of sperm manufactured by the testes drop. The rate at which sexual function drops off is very unpredictable. For some males, it may occur rapidly, particularly when other medical problems are present. Others may retain their ability to function sexually, and even sire children, into their eighties and nineties.

For many men, andropause is associated with significant changes in emotional well-being. Their sense of virility and manhood may be threatened by their inability to perform sexually. They may become despondent or even depressed. Concern about the possible loss of sexual function can even result in a significant mid-life crisis. In an attempt to validate their manhood, some men damage their relationship further by turning their attention to sports or fast cars or by initiating a new—perhaps even illicit—romantic relationship.

Women—Menopause

Menopause is generally a well-demarcated event that is signaled by the cessation of menstrual periods. This occurs when estrogen is no longer made by the ovaries. The average age of menopause onset is fifty.

There are many symptoms associated with menopause besides the loss of menstruation. These may include hot flashes, vaginal dryness, and moodiness. Another obvious consequence is a loss of the ability to reproduce. Some of the symptoms of menopause may begin several years before menstrual periods completely stop, due to a gradual decrease in estrogen production. This period is called perimenopause, and may start in the early forties for some women.

A loss of estrogen causes the blood flow to the genital organs to decrease. This diminishes a woman's ability to experience lubrication during sexual arousal. A lack of lubrication in turn leads to irritation, dryness, bleeding, or pain during sexual intercourse. In addition, long-term estrogen deficiency actually causes the vagina to gradually shrink in size through atrophy. An atrophic vagina has less ability to expand during arousal, eventually making penile penetration difficult or impossible.

Women may also notice a loss of sex drive during menopause and perimenopause. However, this is due to a gradual loss of testosterone, rather than a lack of estrogen. Testosterone is normally manufactured in small amounts by the ovaries in the course of the ovulatory cycle. It helps increase sexual desire, particularly around the most fertile time of the cycle.

Menopause can also be associated with substantial psychological problems. These symptoms are frequently related to a recognition that fertility has passed. It occurs when children may have all moved out of the home, resulting in a sense of loneliness that some call the "empty nest syndrome." Despondency and a lack of purpose may be made worse by mood swings that can be associated with the absence of estrogen. When this happens, women may demonstrate significantly altered behavior. Some admit that they don't even recognize themselves anymore. Depression is also sometimes present.

Again, the good news is that many, if not all, of the physical and emotional consequences of estrogen deficiency can be treated with adequate estrogen replacement. This enables many women to have the desire and ability to remain sexually active until very late in life. Therefore, estrogen replacement therapy is something that every menopausal woman should discuss with her physician.

MEDICAL PROBLEMS

After age fifty, men and women also experience medical problems that can affect sexual function. Diseases of the nervous or circulatory systems are especially injurious to sexual health, since these systems must be intact and function properly for a person to have a normal sexual response. These illnesses include stroke, high blood pressure, spinal cord injuries, multiple sclerosis, and diabetes.

A variety of other physical conditions can cause an individual to be unable to respond sexually in a normal fashion. Any chronic illness, disability, immobilization, or major surgery can cause problems. Arthritis, kidney disease, chronic low back pain, cancer, lung disease, thyroid disease, heart disease, arthritis, and obesity also can negatively affect sexual function. Alcoholism, tobacco use, and disfigurement, such as might occur with a mastectomy or severe injuries, can have this same effect. In addition, mental health problems, such as depression, frequently result in sexual dysfunction.

Heart Attack

Impotence and decreased sexual desire often occur in those who have experienced a heart attack. Studies have estimated that as many as sixty-six to seventy-five percent of men and women have reduced levels of sexual activity following their attacks. This is due primarily to psychogenic factors such as fear, anxiety, misinformation, and depression. However, medications used following heart attacks may also result in sexual dysfunction. Not uncommonly, spouses of heart attack patients may refuse to resume normal sexual activity because of fear that their spouse may be harmed. Physicians used to encourage patients to avoid sexual activity following a heart attack because of a concern that it may cause a second attack. This thought still prevents many from trying to resume normal sexual relations after recovery.

It is now known that the vast majority of heart attack patients can reasonably expect to resume sexual relations without any further problems or risk of a second attack as long as there are not lingering health problems. In the majority of cases, sex can be resumed within four months of the original heart attack. Cardiac rehabilitation programs may also strengthen the heart and facilitate resumption of normal daily activities. When an individual is able to accomplish a designated amount of work, roughly equivalent to climbing a set of stairs briskly without undo strain, he or she may be cleared by the physician to resume sexual activity. Nitroglycerin use prior to sexual activity is prescribed in some cases (although it cannot be taken in conjunction with Viagra). Sometimes the heart is monitored during sexual intercourse to further assess the cardiac status and make appropriate recommendations.

Surgery

Hysterectomy and prostatectomy are among the surgical procedures that can adversely affect an individual's sexual function.

Hysterectomy

A great deal of misinformation exists regarding the effect of hysterectomy on sexual function. A few vocal writers portray hysterectomy as an operation that defeminizes women and diminishes their sexual capacity. Women are encouraged by these "experts" to avoid hysterectomy, especially the removal of ovaries, at all costs.

Surveys of patients, both prospectively and retrospectively, and the experience of most gynecologists, indicate that sexual relations are generally unaffected in the majority of women who undergo hysterectomy (Rinehart, 81). An exception to this would be in cases where a radical hysterectomy for cancer is required. Radical hysterectomy may damage the nervous innervation of the pelvis or create shortening of the vagina. These changes can affect the sexual response. However, most hysterectomies are not of this type.

Interviews of patients who have had hysterectomies show that, in most cases, a woman's sexual experience is unchanged following surgery. Indeed, if any change is evident, women often note an improvement in their ability to enjoy sexual relations after hysterectomy. This may occur for several reasons, including a lack of concern about getting pregnant, no longer having to time sexual relations around menstrual periods, and the absence of pain (if pain was previously present). One study of patients undergoing hysterectomy showed that ninety percent reported no change in their sexual activity after the operation (*see* Huffman).

Women whose ovaries are removed prior to natural menopause will usually experience the rapid onset of what is called surgical menopause. This can cause a decrease in sex drive along with other menopausal symptoms. As with natural menopause, the symptoms of surgical menopause are preventable through the use of hormone replacement therapy. Estrogen replacement allows most women to pass into menopause without any significant sexual adjustment reactions following removal of the ovaries (Rudy, 40). In addition, physicians are becoming increasingly comfortable with prescribing low doses of testosterone to augment a woman's sex drive, especially if the ovaries are removed at a young age.

We should point out that some women do struggle with sexual intimacy following hysterectomy, and some experience sexual dysfunction. However, in many cases, these women either had sexual problems before hysterectomy, have psychological problems that prevent sexual fulfillment, or have major marital problems that contribute to their dysfunction (Rinehart, 81–82).

When a woman has decreased desire or a diminished orgasmic response after hysterectomy, then counseling, empathetic support, appropriate hormone therapy, and the passage of time usually help her return to normal levels of interest and sexual responsiveness. In general, if proper preoperative education is given, if there are no pre-existing sexual problems, and if the woman has a supportive spouse, the negative reactions following hysterectomy are few, even when the ovaries must be removed.

Prostatectomy

Benign prostatic hypertrophy (BPH) is an age-related phenomenon in men. It occurs commonly after age sixty and is present in fifty to seventy-five percent of men age eighty or older. In addition, prostate cancer accounts for fifteen to twenty-two percent of all cancers in men. BPH and cancer may each require surgical removal of the prostate gland. The removal of the prostate gland can result in impotence.

Four different surgical approaches are used to remove, completely or in part, the prostate gland. Transurethral prostatectomy (TURP) is the most commonly utilized technique for prostate gland removal. Impotence due to neurologic damage or disruption of the blood supply to the penis from transurethral prostatectomy is relatively uncommon, occuring in about five percent of cases. Actually, most cases of impotence following TURP are actually psychogenic in origin. Psychogenic impotence stems from fear, ignorance, or other interrelational dynamics associated with the surgery. The degree to which men experience postoperative impotence seems to correlate with the amount of preoperative reassurance and counseling given.

Three other types of prostatectomy exist. They are called supra-pubic, retropubic, and perineal. These operations are associated with higher impotency rates than the transurethral approach, particularly when lymph nodes must be removed in connection with treatment of prostate cancer. If impotence occurs following prostate surgery, a variety of treatments are available. However, treatments for impotence following the more invasive surgeries for prostate removal are not always successful.

MEDICATIONS

A variety of prescription medications can cause sexual dysfunction. These drugs may diminish or completely destroy one or more of the three phases of sexual response—desire, arousal, and orgasm. Some drugs affect the sexual response with regularity and others cause problems only occasionally. The general categories of medications that cause sexual problems are those used for high blood pressure, heart arrythmias, depression, psychiatric disease, seizures, and insomnia. These drugs block or alter the normal physiologic processes the normal sexual response requires. They do this through their actions in the brain, in the smooth muscle of the genitalia, or in the vascular system. The appendix at the end of this book contains a partial list of the most common medications that cause sexual problems.

In addition to prescription drugs, a number of nonprescription drugs can also cause sexual dysfunction. These include niacin, antihistamines, diet pills, and antiulcer drugs such as Tagamet, Zantac, and Pepcid. Many illicit drugs such as barbiturates, amphetamines, cocaine, and heroin likewise cause significant problems with sexual function. Tobacco use or excessive alcohol intake can also cause problems.

PSYCHOLOGICAL FACTORS

Not all sexual problems in the later years of marriage are due to physical deterioration, drugs, or aging. As with younger couples, older marriages are not immune from marital discord, and psychological barriers that prevent fulfilling sexual intimacy may be present. Sometimes these problems have been present for many years; other times they develop later. One's perception of the aging process itself can be a late-evolving psychological barrier. Some individuals may not accept the fact that aging detracts from their appearance; others may be disappointed because their spouse's physical appearance has changed. These perceptions may hinder sexual desire, limit arousal, or prevent orgasm. Obviously, if present, psychological issues must be addressed for the couple to enjoy physical intimacy in the golden years of life.

CHAPTER 12

Treating Sexual Dysfunction
in the Later Years

Ralph was discouraged. When he looked at himself in the mirror, he saw an old man with a pot belly and a bald head. He looked just like his dad used to look—worn and tired. He had promised himself that he would never let himself get that way; he was going to stay young and maintain his vitality. But, in spite of his hopes, he wasn't what he imagined he would turn out to be at his age. He couldn't understand why his wife, Judy, still loved him.

Of course he didn't want to talk to anybody, least of all Judy, about what was bothering him the most. He couldn't even say the word out loud. Impotence. It described how he felt about his life in general, not just his inability to function properly in the bedroom.

When it first started, he had tried to make light of it with a lame joke or comment, and Judy had been very good about it. As the problem became more common, he would pretend like nothing had happened, or mumble a weak apology before drifting off to sleep. Now he just avoided sex altogether. He was glad Judy didn't bring up the subject, because he wasn't sure he could handle it. He felt that he was a failure.

A COMMON PROBLEM

Sexual dysfunction occurs with increasing frequency as men and women pass age fifty. This is often a consequence of the effects of age, illness, and medications. Virtually every couple experiences at least some minor sexual problems in the later years. Historically, many older couples have sadly resigned themselves to celibacy during this period of their lives.

Fortunately, with the advances of medical science, husbands and wives can continue to function normally and enjoy the by-products of an enriching sex life to a much greater extent than previous generations. The vast majority of couples now can continue to experience the joy and benefits of sexual intimacy until late in their lives.

MALE SEXUAL DYSFUNCTION

The treatment of male sexual difficulties in the later years begins with a complete evaluation by a physician. This is particularly true because so many male problems at this time of life have a physical basis. A doctor can determine if there are medical and drug-related causes of sexual dysfunction so that appropriate steps can be taken.

With the ready availability of a large number of products for the treatment of male sexual dysfunction, people may be tempted to self-treat before the problem has been medically evaluated. But no single treatment will correct all problems, and there are side effects and risks that must be considered. Therefore, it is best to find out what the specific problem is and allow the treatment to be tailored by a doctor.

With the advent of Viagra, erectile dysfunction has gained greater public awareness. It has been discussed frankly on television. News specials and magazine articles review the subject frequently. And "erectile dysfunction" has become a part of our vocabulary. All of this is helpful since impotence is a significant problem that people have historically been reluctant to address openly. Now that there is greater public recognition of the problem, men appear less hesitant to broach the issue with their physicians.

Viagra

Viagra is the trade name for Sildenafil. It is the first of what will undoubtedly be many orally administered drugs for the treatment of impotence. It causes the relaxation of smooth muscle (specifically the corpus cavernosum muscle cells of the penis) that is essential for the development of an erection.

Viagra is effective for the treatment of impotence that occurs from both psychological and physical causes. What makes Viagra most appealing is that erection occurs in response to sexual stimulation, not independent of it. Therefore, the erectile response is more natural. Men report an increased ability to obtain an adequate erection, increased orgasm, and increased satisfaction with their sexual experience, although sexual desire is not enhanced. Success rates in the seventy to eighty percent range have been reported, depending upon the dose of medication used. The wives of patients using Viagra also report improved sexual satisfaction due to their husband's increased ability to consummate sexual relations.

Of course, there is no such thing as a medication without side effects. This is true of Viagra as well. Headaches, flushing, heartburn, visual disturbance, and inflammation of the nasal passages are the most commonly noted side effects. Viagra can also cause engorgement and severe pain in the penis due to a prolonged erection—a condition called priapism. It should not be taken if there is an anatomic deformity of the penis or by persons who have retinitis pigmentosa. Viagra can also cause serious complications in men taking nitroglycerin. Therefore, Viagra and nitroglycerin should never be prescribed or taken at the same time. Finally, there have been a few cases of heart attack among older patients with a type of heart disease that causes low blood flow to the heart muscle when they resumed sexual activity with the help of Viagra. These side effects can often be minimized by a reduction of the dosage. Thus, Viagra should never be taken without first consulting a physician.

Yohimbine

Yohimbine is another medication that can be taken orally. It is derived from the bark of the yohimbine tree in Africa. However, some studies suggest no improvement in sexual function, while others show that it increases sexual desire and successfully treats erectile disorders a high percentage of the time. It may primarily benefit those who have a psychological cause for impotence, thus explaining why studies show mixed results.

Testosterone

Testosterone, and a large number of testosterone-like substances, are available over the counter and by prescription. These have been touted as treatments for low sexual desire and impotence. However, objective studies have not shown a consistent benefit from the use of testosterone and other androgens in men whose testosterone levels are already in the normal range for their age. Over-the-counter and non-prescription agents that claim to increase testosterone levels have not been rigorously studied, despite claims to the contrary. Presumably, since testosterone administration results in no definite improvement in the sexual function of men with normal testosterone levels, these agents will not result in any improvement either. In addition, the use of androgens can have serious long-term side effects. In men, they can cause atrophy of the testicles, breast enlargement, excessive and frequent penile erections, liver problems, nausea, fluid retention, and lower sperm counts. Most of these side effects are related to the dose of testosterone taken, and do not occur as frequently when taken in low doses.

Intracavernosal Injections

In the 1980's, medications were developed for direct injection into the corpora cavernosa muscle of the penis. These proved to be very effective, but with the development of the oral agents now available, their popularity has waned. However, intracavernosal injections are still used by some men.

The intracavernosal injections use very tiny needles, and discomfort from the injections is usually minimal. The medications include papaverine hydrochloride, phentolamine mesylate, and prostaglandin E1. All of these agents are very effective and result in a high degree of patient satisfaction. Side effects may include prolonged erections, discomfort from injections, penile pain, the formation of small nodules around the injection sites, infection, bruising, liver function problems, and lightheadedness.

Despite the high degree of satisfaction with intracavernosal injections, some patients are uncomfortable or embarrassed by having to inject a medication into the muscle of the penis. Some feel it is unnatural, since erections occur without sexual stimulation. Others are concerned about side effects. Studies show that about half the men who use intracavernosal injections stop its use before twelve months.

Transurethril Alprostadil

Alprostadil is a synthetic prostaglandin agent. Prostaglandins are chemicals that are naturally manufactured by the body and have many important effects, including a role in the development of penile erections. Alprostadil comes in a tiny pellet that is inserted into the end of the urethra. The medication is absorbed into the blood stream, and then returns via the blood stream to the penis.

In one study, sixty-five percent of impotent men using transurethral alprostadil were able to consummate intercourse at least once using the medication. Side effects included penile pain, discomfort or injury of the penis due to application of the medication into the urethra, and dizziness. Notwithstanding these problems, it is easier to use and is associated with fewer side effects compared to intracavernosal injections.

Vacuum Erection Devices

Vacuum devices are a relatively unsophisticated, but safe and effective, means of producing erections in men. These devices include a wide variety of apparatuses that became available in the early 1980s, but whose use has diminished since the advent of other options. Another reason for the somewhat infrequent use of vacuum devices is the perception of doctors and patients that they are unnatural and unscientific compared to medications. However, many patients report a high degree of satisfaction with their use.

Essentially, all vacuum devices work the same way. A vacuum is used to draw blood into the penis to create an erection. Then a constriction device is placed at the base of the penis to maintain the erection. The most common side effects are bruising of the penis, pain, numbness, injury, and blocked or painful ejaculation. With success rates of ninety percent, patients who discontinue its use usually do so because of the cumbersome nature of some vacuum devices, the "unnaturalness" of the process, unwanted side effects, a lack of manual dexterity required to operate the apparatus, or the failure to produce an adequate erection.

Penile Prosthesis

Penile implants are synthetic rods or inflatable devices that are surgically implanted in the corpora cavernosa of the penis. They make the penis rigid and allow for consummation of sexual relations. Some implants leave the penis in a permanently stiffened condition; others can be inflated prior to intercourse. Implants can only be removed surgically and are more expensive than other methods of treatment for impotence. Despite these drawbacks, eighty percent of men who have implants say they would have the operation a second time. Again, penile prostheses are used less today because of the development of other methods.

Naturopathic Aids

A wide array of "natural" agents are marketed as aids to sexual function. These can usually be obtained without a physician's prescription. The naturopathic aids claim to do everything from enhancing sexual desire, to restoring potency, to prolonging erections, to creating more intense orgasms—seemingly without side effects or complications. However, despite their claims, there is a lack of proof that they work or are totally safe. This is because food supplements, vitamins, and herbal remedies are not subject to the same research and testing as prescription medications.

Through careful phrasing, those who market natural products create the image that they are tested and proven, but usually they are not. However, some benefit may be derived from natural agents because of the placebo effect. This means that when a person takes something that he or she thinks will help, it often does, even if it is an empty pill.

FEMALE SEXUAL DYSFUNCTION

In the later years of marriage, women may notice two negative changes in their sexual response: a lower sexual desire and more discomfort with sexual intercourse. Both of these changes are usually caused by a lack of hormones. The lower sex drive is usually due to lower testosterone levels. The discomfort of intercourse is commonly due to estrogen deficiency.

Hormone Replacement in Menopausal Women

It has been found that most symptoms of menopause, including a loss of sexual desire and genital tract atrophy, can be treated successfully through hormone replacement therapy (HRT). HRT may consist of one, two, or three hormones. They are 1) estrogen, which can be taken in a variety of ways, 2) progesterone, for those who still have a uterus (to protect it against cancer), and, 3) testosterone, for those who need an additional boost to their sex drive. When HRT is taken, women often report their desire for sexual intimacy is maintained at or near premenopausal levels. In addition, sexual function is maintained, particularly the ability to consummate sexual intercourse without pain. Those who cannot take estrogen, and those who still experience vaginal dryness despite HRT, may be helped by using commercial lubricants.

Surveys of menopausal women indicate that satisfaction with sexual intimacy is actually quite high during the later years when HRT is taken. Women report a normal or near-normal sexual desire and are able to have sexual relations without undue discomfort. It may take longer for women to become aroused and experience orgasm, and the orgasms may be less intense, but despite these changes, sexual activity continues to be a fulfilling and important aspect of the marriage relationship despite advancing years. For these reasons, if no other problems exist, a woman can anticipate that she can remain sexually active as long as she wishes if HRT is taken.

Hormone replacement therapy, especially estrogen use, also has other proven benefits. It successfully treats hot flashes, mood swings, and depression associated with menopause. To be free of these symptoms alone can increase sexual desire. Estrogen also prevents the development of osteoporosis and heart disease and may even be effective in preventing Alzheimer's Disease. For these reasons, almost all physicians advocate the use of estrogen in menopausal women.

However, not all women are candidates for estrogen therapy. Women with a history of a venous blood clot, a blood clot in the lung, uterine cancer, breast cancer, liver disease, and stroke are probably not candidates for HRT, although exceptions are made in some cases. Fortunately, the vast majority of women do not have these problems and are, therefore, not restricted from taking estrogen. Side effects of testosterone in women include the growth of hair on the face and other body parts, enlargement of the clitoris, partial baldness, and acne, although at low doses, these side effects are not common.

It has been suggested that Viagra may benefit women who suffer from arousal disorders and anorgasmia. As of this date, preliminary studies have shown that about twenty percent of women respond to its use. However, Viagra studies in large numbers of women are now underway. These studies are needed in order to show that it produces significant improvement beyond placebo levels and to better understand the side effects in women. Therefore, at this point in time, Viagra cannot be recommended for women, but this may change as further research is done.

FINAL NOTE

Under normal circumstances, most couples are able to enjoy wonderful marital intimacy until late in life. However, the husband and wife may need to alter their expectations to avoid disappointment. Sexual interaction between older spouses is usually not as frequent as earlier in marriage. Additionally, the physical response may not be as intense and both husband and wife may need more time to reach full arousal and orgasm. Nonetheless, marital intimacy should be enjoyable and emotionally fulfilling in the majority of relationships. Surveys of couples in their later years indicate this is the case.

Unfortunately, there are couples who completely discontinue all sexual relations in the later years even though they would rather not. This occurs most often because of male sexual dysfunction. Frequently the husband declares the subject off-limits, and the issue is never discussed because of ignorance, fear, or pride. This leaves the wife disappointed, frustrated, and even angry. She may incorrectly conclude that her husband no longer loves her.

This does not need to happen. Help is now available for problems that were previously considered untreatable. The most common problems—impotence and lack of desire in men, and vaginal atrophy and lack of desire in women—can be cured, or at least significantly remedied. All that is required is a willingness to address the problems and seek medical help.

CHAPTER 13

Some Thoughts for Husbands

This chapter is personally addressed to husbands. We want to summarize some of the ideas from earlier chapters that we think will help you meet the spiritual, emotional, and physical needs of your wife. These principles, when understood and applied in the context of marriage, will enhance marital intimacy for you and your wife.

IT TAKES TWO TO GAIN ETERNAL LIFE

Exaltation is available only to husbands and wives, a man and a woman who love each other dearly. The Plan of Salvation clearly teaches that alone, neither of you is really complete. Recall President Boyd K. Packer's statement: "No man receives the fullness of the priesthood [in the temple] without a woman at his side (D&C 131:1–4). . . . She is there beside him in that sacred place. She shares in all that he receives. . . . The man cannot ascend to the highest ordinances—the sealing ordinances—without her," (*Ensign*, May 1998, 73).

When you married in the temple, the two of you entered into the new and everlasting covenant of marriage (D&C 131:1–4). We do that, as Elder Bruce R. McConkie taught us, to "create for ourselves eternal family units of our own, patterned after the family of God our Heavenly Father," (*Ensign* May, 1982, 34). The gospel of Jesus Christ points us all toward marriage and family. Its principles are most meaningful to married companions, husbands and wives who serve each other. In so doing, they find their souls enlarged and their talents magnified. Ultimately they develop a oneness that qualifies them for eternal life. The greatest of God's blessings are reserved for righteous men and women sealed in the temple by the Holy Spirit of Promise (D&C 132:19–20).

Though a temple marriage provides the setting for the sealing power to be exercised in your behalf, that ceremony, by itself, will not exalt you. To quote Elder Robert D. Hales: "An eternal bond doesn't just happen as a result of sealing covenants we make in the temple. . . . To receive the blessings . . . that our Heavenly Father has given to us, we have to keep the commandments and conduct ourselves in such a way that our families *will want to live with us* in the eternities," (*Ensign*, 1996:65, emphasis added). Attaining the highest degree of glory in the Celestial Kingdom requires that both of you unite your spiritual, emotional, mental, and physical endowments in a way that complement each other and make you want to be eternal companions.

In marriage, your wife gave her consent to be your sweetheart, your lover, your companion, your confidante, and the mother of your children—not just for this life, but forever! In return, you pledged the same things and promised your fidelity, giving your commitment to do your best as her husband and as the father of her children. These are sacred trusts, responsibilities that cannot be fulfilled casually or without considerable effort on your part.

God endowed his daughters with traits that can make them wonderful wives. Your wife's personality, demeanor, and talents may be very different from yours, but they are naturally complementary. Women were fashioned by God to become the mortal mothers of His spirit children, and they are given special abilities that allow them to fulfill their divine nature. The Savior explained the role of women in the Father's Plan to the Prophet Joseph Smith: "For [she is] given unto [her husband] to multiply and replenish the earth, according to my commandment, and to fulfill the promise which was given by my Father before the foundation of the world, and for [her] exaltation in the eternal worlds, that [she] may bear the souls of men; for herein is the work of my Father continued, that he may be glorified" (D&C 132:63). For women, the roles of wife and mother are emphasized more than any others in the scriptures.

Sadly, we acknowledge that many women are not treated in a manner that befits their importance in the Father's Plan. Some are treated in the home and the workplace in ways that diminish their sense of worth. Others are placed in positions where their feminine natures never fully bloom. Unfortunately, women are often viewed in worldly environs as little more than sex objects or mere housekeepers, a most offensive perception to righteous men and women.

Women who choose to be home with their children are frequently looked upon as inferior to those who leave the hearth to go into the workplace. Hopefully, they find comfort in the words of Elder Richard G. Scott: "Of course, as a woman you can do exceptionally well in the workplace, but is that the best use of your divinely appointed talents and feminine traits?" (*Ensign*, November 1996, 74).

As a woman comes to understand her divine role in the Father's Plan (while resisting the prevailing "winds of doctrine" that swirl about her), she needs your help and encouragement as her companion. It is evident that a caring, supportive, and unselfish husband can enhance a woman's dignity and reinforce her worth as a daughter of God as no one else can. On the other hand, how very destructive to a wife's feelings of adequacy is a husband who is sarcastic, bitter, negative, or critical of her and her efforts as a wife and mother. Wo to the man who offends one of God's faithful daughters! Jacob denounced the careless and wicked husbands of his day: "Ye have broken the hearts of your tender wives, and lost the confidence of your children, because of your bad examples before them; and the sobbings of their hearts ascend up to God against you. And because of the strictness of the word of God, which cometh down against you, many hearts died, pierced with deep wounds," (Jacob 2:35).

Men will stand accountable to God for how they treat their wives and children. On one occasion, President David O. McKay taught a group of Church employees:

> Let me assure you, brethren, that some day you will have a personal priesthood interview with the Savior himself. If you are interested, I will tell you the order in which he will ask you to account for your earthly

responsibilities: First, He will request an accountability report about *your relationship with your wife.* Have you actively been engaged in making her happy and ensuring that her needs have been met as an individual? Second, He will want an accountability report about each of your children individually, information about your relationship to each and every child." (Fred Baker, "Stewardship," emphasis added.)

MEETING THE SPIRITUAL NEEDS OF YOUR WIFE

The Proclamation on the Family declares that "by divine design, fathers are to preside over their families in love and righteousness and are responsible to provide the necessities of life and the protection of their families." You, by priesthood assignment, preside in a "patriarchal quorum." This means that you are to provide leadership by ensuring that family rituals take place—family prayer, family home evening, scripture study, blessing your children, and others. Occasionally, you need to step back and observe your family enterprise from an objective standpoint to consider its strengths and weaknesses. Then you should step forward to do your utmost to influence these special spirits along the path to eternal life. With your wife as your counselor, you direct and assist the "quorum" to become an eternal family unit. Strong and capable leadership is required to bring your family back to God. Leadership means doing what needs to be done for the welfare of your family. After all, the plan calls for you and your wife to someday preside over and govern more than those of your own mortal family (thus the need for future kings and queens, priests and priestesses).

The Lord gave this caution to men who bear the priesthood: "We have learned by sad experience that it is the nature and disposition of almost all men, as soon as they get a little authority, as they suppose, they will immediately begin to exercise unrighteous dominion," (D&C 121:39). Never imagine that your priesthood ordination was authorization to be a tyrant or a boss. Don't use the power of God to demand that family members comply with your wishes. Fathers are to be teachers. They are to be leaders—not drill sergeants. You are to bless and lift, not command or demand. It is the priesthood of Jesus

Christ you hold, and the model He presented was one of being willing to give his life for His Father's family. Hopefully, you feel the same about your wife and children. "No power or influence can or ought to be maintained by virtue of the priesthood," said the Lord to Joseph Smith, "only by persuasion, by long-suffering, by gentleness and meekness, and by love unfeigned; By kindness, and pure knowledge, which shall greatly enlarge the soul," (D&C 121:39, 41–42). Speaking of the need to lead with love, President Spencer W. Kimball gave this counsel to husbands:

> A woman would have no fears of being imposed upon nor of any dictatorial measures nor of any improper demands if the husband is self-sacrificing and worthy. Certainly no sane woman would hesitate to give submission to her own really righteous husband in everything. We are sometimes shocked to see the wife take over the leadership, naming the one to pray, the place to be, the things to do. Husbands are commanded: "love your wives, even as Christ also loved the church, and gave himself for it," (Ephesians 5:25). Here is the answer: Christ loved the Church and its people so much that he voluntarily endured persecution for them, suffered humiliating indignities for them, stoically withstood pain and physical abuse for them, and finally gave his precious life for them. When the husband is ready to treat his household in that manner, not only the wife, but also all the family will respond to his leadership. Certainly, if fathers are to be respected, they must merit respect; if they are to be loved, they must be consistent, lovable, understanding, and kind, and must honor their priesthood. (Kimball, "Home Training," 514.)

Your duty, then, is to serve your family in such a way that they cherish your loving leadership. Women and children are usually more than willing to follow a righteous husband and father, one who is kind and charitable.

Men are often stereotyped as tough, macho, insensitive creatures unaware of the needs and feelings of women and children. Let's destroy that stereotype. Your wife wants you to be tender and sensitive to her and her children's needs. Pray for success in your efforts.

To succeed as the patriarch in your home, you will be driven to your knees many times seeking divine guidance in behalf of your family. Fast Sundays are good opportunities for you to seek special guidance. Never cease trying to influence your family members to be better. "In this life a father is never released from his responsibility," said Elder H. Burke Peterson. "We call bishops, and they serve for a time and are released. Stake presidents likewise are called, serve, and are released. But a father's calling is an eternal calling if he lives worthily," (*Ensign*, November 1977, 87).

MEETING THE EMOTIONAL NEEDS OF YOUR WIFE

Your wife needs your support to deal with the challenges of her great stewardship of motherhood: childbirth, care giving, midnight feedings, colicky babies, cranky toddlers, limited funds, time demands, and challenging teenagers. She must feel loved and appreciated by you to gain a sense of adequacy. When she feels love and appreciation, her resolve and ability to do all that is required increases. President Ezra Taft Benson gave this perspective:

> "Thou shalt love thy wife with all thy heart, and shalt cleave unto her and none else,"(D&C 42:22). To my knowledge there is only one other thing in all scripture that we are commanded to love with all our hearts, and that is God Himself. Think what that means! This kind of love can be shown for your wives in so many ways. First and foremost, nothing except God Himself takes priority over your wife in your life—not work, not recreation, not hobbies. Your wife is your precious, eternal helpmate— your companion. What does it mean to love someone with all your heart? It means to love with all your emotional feelings and with all your devotion. Surely when you love your wife with all your heart, you cannot demean her, criticize her, find fault with her, or abuse her by words, sullen behavior, or actions.
>
> What does it mean to "cleave unto her"? It means to stay close to her, to be loyal and faithful to her, to communicate with her, and to express your love for her. Love means being sensitive to her feelings and needs. She wants

to be noticed and treasured. She wants to be told that you view her as lovely and attractive and important to you. . . . You should be grateful that she is the mother of your children and the queen of your home, grateful that she has chosen . . . to bear, to nourish, to love, and to train your children—as the noblest calling of all. . . . Flowers on special occasions are wonderful, but so is your willingness to help with the dishes, change diapers, get up with a crying child in the night, and leave the television or the newspaper to help with the dinner. Those are the quiet ways we say "I love you" with our actions. They bring rich dividends for such little effort. (*Ensign,* November 1987, 49–50.)

As a husband, there are probably two areas where you can immediately improve your marriage: 1) Willingly and cheerfully help with housework responsibilities; and 2) willingly and cheerfully increase your involvement as a father. When you are home, *be home* in both body and spirit! The twin tasks of housework and fathering, done cheerfully and voluntarily, will dramatically increase your wife's positive feelings for you. Here is how one wife put it: "I love it when my husband comes home from school and instead of complaining about the house and the kids, gives me a big hug and kiss and asks me how my day went and if there is anything that he can do to help, not in a condescending way, or in a way that makes me feel that I have not been very effective in keeping the children's toys put away, but in a way that I really feel like he cares and wants to help me." This kind of sensitivity lifts spirits and relieves the emotional burdens that wives carry as homemakers and mothers.

Your wife needs to feel total trust and fidelity in her relationship with you. She needs to know that you love her more than anyone or anything else, and that you are willing to put her needs first, even before those of the children. We hear wives who say, "I am about number four on his list. First comes golf, then work, then church, and then maybe me." Your first duty is to strengthen your relationship with her. Sometimes this means that you sacrifice to be with her, or that you support her opinion over that of your children or other adults.

Along these same lines, you must not do anything that would cause your wife to question your fidelity. You may have had many relationships with female friends before marriage where strong emotional bonds existed. Such relationships are now out of order. Of course you have female friends, but that is what they are: friends. In the workplace you often work closely with other women. Keep your associations totally professional. Do not share confidences or problems in your marriage with anyone else. Your wife is your confidante and you betray her trust when you are emotionally intimate with another woman.

Finally, your wife values financial security. She needs to know that there are sufficient funds to operate the family enterprise. She needs the economic part of marriage to function smoothly in order to feel comfortable. She wants to be with a husband who is hardworking and industrious. As the provider, you must do all that you can to ensure that your family's temporal needs are met, even if you have to take a second job to provide them. Avoid the temptation to send your wife into the workplace. Children are too precious to be left to the care of outsiders. They have been reserved to come forth in these latter days to perform a great work in the Kingdom of God.

Church leaders have counseled men in our day to be the providers for their families so that their wives can be mothers. What a tremendous load some women carry because they must not only work outside the home, but they must also perform the major share of child care and household work and church callings and other civic duties. Elder Richard G. Scott addressed this issue: "As a husband, don't encourage your wife to go to work to help in your divinely appointed responsibility of providing resources for the family, if you can possibly avoid it. As the prophets have counseled, to the extent possible with the help of the Lord, as parents, work together to keep Mother in the home," (*Ensign*, November 1996, 74). Of course, if you and your wife have agreed that she must work for financial sustenance, be sure to increase your performance of household and parental duties.

MEETING THE PHYSICAL NEEDS OF YOUR WIFE

You have an opportunity to make sexual relations a good experience for your wife. This is as much a part of your stewardship as her spouse and companion as it is to provide for her spiritual, financial, and emotional well-being. It is a responsibility that you must approach with care and humility. Your wife has sexual feelings and needs that may be different from your own, something you will come to understand. For example, men are not as likely to separate love and sex as do women. Husbands don't just want to settle for a hug, a kiss, a cuddle on the couch, or to just hold a wife in a tender embrace. They want to be sexually intimate. For wives, however, expressing love doesn't always mean sexual relations. Sometimes it just means being held, being close physically, being touched affectionately, or being understood. We hear some sad comments from unhappy wives: "I think that sex is the only reason he married me." "As long as he can have sex, he treats me nicely." "When he can't have sex he is very difficult to live with. He keeps asking 'how many more days do we have to wait?'"

There will be many times in your marriage when you will need to exercise self-restraint. If there is a plea we would make to husbands, it is this: If you genuinely love your wife for her spiritual and emotional attributes as well as her physical endowments, demonstrate your love for her on occasions by sacrificing your own desires to be intimate. There will be days when your wife has had a difficult time with the children, faced a number of emotional challenges, or is simply too exhausted to respond. If you will treat her as your companion and sweetheart, and show consideration for her needs and feelings, and if she is healthy and rested, you will find that your intimate times together will be enjoyable and fulfilling.

Intimacy cannot be demanded or manipulated. Sexual relations must be an unforced mutual expression of love. "Husband and wife...are authorized, in fact they are commanded, to have proper sex when they are properly married for time and eternity," said President Spencer W. Kimball. "That does not mean that we need to go to great extremes. That does not mean that a woman is the servant of her husband. It does not mean that any man has a right to demand sex anytime that he might want it. He should be reasonable and understanding and it should be a general program between the two, so they understand and everybody is happy about it," (*Teachings*, p. 312).

We have observed that wives married to kind and gentle husbands and fathers *are* interested in sex and do not seek to avoid it. Women who are accused by their husbands of being uninterested in sex or wives who profess that sex is only for the purpose of having children are often women who have been mistreated by their husbands. It is not necessary to read letters to advice columnists to understand this point. When you put your wife and children first in your life, the intimate side of marriage becomes an enriching, voluntary gift your wife will gladly share with you to strengthen and lift your union above the profane and mundane things of life.

Another stereotype often attributed to men is that they are well-informed about sexual matters. In reality, they are usually quite uninformed, particularly about the biology and psychology of sexual intimacy. If this is true for you, you may need to do some study and research. That is a primary incentive for this book. It can be helpful to study some basic anatomy and physiology, for sure, but don't forget, more importantly, to study your wife as well. If you focus attention on her needs and responses, she will be your marriage guide. Ask her to tell you what she is feeling and what activities help her to respond. She may be reluctant to make suggestions because she doesn't want to come across as being critical.

A common tendency for a husband during sexual intimacy is to think that his wife is feeling the same level of sexual arousal he is. He assumes that because he is aroused, so is his wife, when the truth may be that her mind is miles away on the children, an event of the day, a Relief Society lesson, or a leaky faucet! Work on learning to "read" her and getting her to share her feelings with you, and you will have fewer disappointments. A wife expressed these sentiments about her husband who understood her varying moods and needs:

> *It is so important for a husband to make a wife feel loved all the time. My husband is so good at this. He understands that sometimes I just need to be held and he'll have to wait until another time to be intimate. He is very sensitive to my needs and so good at reading my signals even when I don't just come out and say what I'm feeling—although I'm sure life would be much easier for both of us if I could just learn to do that. Even though I try to be clear and don't expect him to read my mind, I'm sure I'm still confusing to him because I'm a woman and he's a man. He is so patient and understanding*

with me. He is affectionate outside the bedroom and that makes me feel loved and cared for all the time, which makes me more willing to meet his desire for intimacy.

Of all the points mentioned in Chapter 4 regarding the female sexual response, we wish to re-emphasize two here. First, the time required for your wife to reach orgasm is most likely going to be longer than for you. It may require up to a half hour of gentle touching and stimulation for her to reach sexual climax, whereas you are capable of physical fulfillment in a fraction of that time. Don't be selfish or impatient in this matter. A woman is much like a fine violin that needs tuning before it can bring forth its greatest melodies. Go slowly and take whatever time she needs to find fulfillment.

Second, most women do not experience orgasm without clitoral stimulation. That will be your responsibility, consistent with her feelings and desires, of course. You will probably need your wife's help to learn how to provide such stimulation. The clitoris is an organ whose sole function is to provide sexual arousal and pleasure for your wife when touched in a stimulating manner during sexual activity. You may find that in sexual intercourse your wife does not receive sufficient stimulation. Therefore, you may need to experiment together to find ways to provide the stimulation your wife needs to achieve orgasm. This may include altering positions or placing a pillow under your wife's back or providing very gentle manual stimulation for her if she finds it helpful and enjoyable. This, of course, is a very private matter that every married couple must work out, but we mention it here since the lack of clitoral stimulation is one of the most common reasons why a woman does not experience a climax during sexual intercourse.

Perhaps this is the place to explain that sometimes we find couples who believe that to stimulate a spouse manually is a form of masturbation. We want to clarify that masturbation is *self*-stimulation for the purpose of bringing self-orgasm or ejaculation. It is a completely selfish act. The dangers of this practice have been the subject of a number of writings by Church authorities. But in marriage, using a finger or the hand for gentle touching and mutual arousal is an essential part of the sexual experience. It is *not* masturbation when you stimulate her (or she you). Indeed, this may be exactly what she needs from you to help her reach a heightened sense of passion that allows her to experience the orgasm phase of the sexual response.

SUMMARY

As your sweetheart's husband, you are responsible to be the best companion and father you can be. You have the vital and even sacred duty to help meet your wife's spiritual, emotional, and physical needs. This can be accomplished with some basic information on sexual matters and by interacting with your wife in a tender, Christlike manner. When you do so, your wife will be more interested in responding to and meeting your needs for intimacy. Women enjoy being treated kindly and respectfully. They find it difficult to give themselves fully to a spouse who does not appreciate them or to a husband who is abrupt, distant, unkind, or critical. They enjoy the company of a husband who treats them as an equal, who safeguards their feelings, and who does not seek sexual intimacy simply for self-gratification. We are confident that as you approach physical intimacy with sensitivity and concern for all facets of her life, you will find greater fulfillment in this important area of your marriage. Remember, you are in your marriage together. Elder Richard G. Scott stated:

> In the Lord's plan, it takes two—a man and a woman—to form a whole. Indeed, a husband and wife are not two identical halves, but a wondrous, divinely determined combination of complementary capacities and characteristics. Marriage allows these different characteristics to come together in oneness—in unity—to bless a husband and wife, their children and grandchildren. For the greatest happiness and productivity in life, both husband and wife are needed. Their efforts interlock and are complementary. Each has individual traits that best fit the role the Lord has defined for happiness as a man or woman. When used as the Lord intends, those capacities allow a married couple to think, act, and rejoice as one—to face challenges together and overcome them as one, to grow in love and under-

standing, and through temple ordinances to be bound together as one whole, eternally. That is the plan. (*Ensign,* Nov. 1996, 74.)

CHAPTER 14

Some Thoughts for Wives

This chapter addresses some specific ideas that you as a wife might consider as you seek to improve the intimate side of your marriage. We want to review a few important principles that can help you create greater spiritual, emotional, and physical oneness with your husband.

ETERNAL LIFE: HUSBANDS AND WIVES HELPING EACH OTHER

It is no more possible for a woman to obtain exaltation by herself than it is for a man to do so alone. Elder Bruce R. McConkie stated: "If righteous men have power through the gospel and its crowning ordinance of celestial marriage to become kings and priests to rule in exaltation forever, it follows that the women by their side (without whom they cannot attain exaltation) will be queens and priestesses (Rev. 1:6; 5:10). Exaltation grows out of the eternal union of a man and his wife," (*Mormon Doctrine*, 613). Your husband is an important key to your eternal happiness. As imperfect as he may be right now, he is the one with whom you will serve as a queen and priestess in the hereafter. In order for your husband to realize his greatest potential and thereby ensure the eternal progression of both of you, you must help him rise to his greatest spiritual stature.

Husbands and fathers carry many burdens. By divine decree, your husband is required to lead in spiritual matters, provide temporally for the family, and meet a variety of demands that come to him through his career, church service, and civic responsibilities. He does this with your capable assistance, to be certain, but the load he carries can sometimes be heavy. We have great admiration for the fact that so many men pull off these duties so well. It is especially laudatory when they do so without compromising values or losing sight of priorities, despite the temptations and unholy influences that abound in the media and workplaces of the world.

Your husband has never been a husband before. Never, in all of eternity, has he been married or challenged by the responsibilities that are now placed upon him by your union. His marriage to you now is his first opportunity to learn how to be a husband and father. He will make mistakes as he struggles to do that which is required of him. Because of this, he needs and appreciates your understanding and will be grateful for your forgiveness when he falls short in his attempts to do his best.

Husbands learn about manhood, priesthood, and fulfilling their duties by watching and listening to other good men—fathers, brothers, and priesthood leaders. However, women also have a great impact on their development. Who can doubt the inestimable value of a loving mother, or a kind sister, or a supportive wife? Indeed, in the most important tasks of life, a woman is her husband's helpmate and gentle tutor. Through whom else can he so completely learn to be an eternal companion, a role that he will eventually have for eternity?

A righteous wife brings out the best in her husband. She inspires him to want to do well because of his desire to please her. Sometimes pride and vanity get in his way, but a man is usually willing to learn from a kind and loving wife who can gently shape him into an effective companion and father. In order to help him be effective in his roles, a wife must retain a vision of what she knows her husband is capable of becoming and help strengthen his positive attributes. (This is one reason you might want to read each other's patriarchal blessings occasionally.) Conversely, when a wife becomes her husband's critic, when she tries to remake him into her father or some other ideal known only to her, then she is no longer a catalyst for positive change in his life.

MEETING THE SPIRITUAL NEEDS OF YOUR HUSBAND

Although men are given the responsibility to lead in spiritual matters, a righteous man understands the importance of a capable and helpful companion. Men don't necessarily desire or relish their roles as the presiding leader in the home; it is not something they necessarily seek. But they also know they cannot shirk their God-given duty. They greatly value a wife who is supportive and allows them to step forward. As a companion, your duty is to kindly remind and encourage your husband in his spiritual responsibilities. At times you may be assigned to lead in certain areas of the marriage where your talents are stronger, but you should never try to take his place as patriarch and priesthood leader. It will be hard for him to be receptive and loving to you if you are pushy or domineering or if you attempt to usurp his role.

Praying together is a prime example of where your influence can be helpful. Sometimes husbands will allow joint prayer to be set aside, especially if personal and family prayer are taking place. But, don't let prayer together slip from your marriage. You simply must keep that tradition going, for it is the way you see into each other's heart. When couples have difficulties in marriage, we have noticed that praying together is the first practice that suffers. The loss of emotional and physical intimacy is then usually not far behind! Sometimes prayer is avoided because of the unrepentant and ill-mannered behavior of one or both spouses. Who wants to kneel down and pray with a spouse who has been unduly critical and sarcastic of them? If this has happened in your marriage, repentance is overdue. Encourage the move back to praying together as a couple.

Although you do not hold the priesthood, your stewardship is just as important as that of your husband. Its dimensions are far different from his. President James E. Faust declared:

> For the daughters of God, doing the Savior's work does not, of course, include the use of the priesthood keys, authority, or power. But it does include building faith by testimony and example. It includes teaching the doctrines of salvation. It includes following the Savior's example of love for all mankind. It includes ministering to others. (James E. Faust, "Relief Society," 94.)

It is your right and prerogative to discover what spiritual talents and gifts you have, and then to blend those strengths with those of your husband in furthering your relationship and guiding your children. Be assured that your husband appreciates your spiritual traits even though he may not always remember to express his thanks for that which you provide. Elder Richard G. Scott made this observation:

> I often interview strong priesthood leaders. When these men speak of their wives, it is with deep tenderness and obvious appreciation. Often, tears flow. Their comments include, "She is more spiritual, purer, and more committed than I," "She motivates me to be a better person," "She is the strength of my life," and "I couldn't do it without her." As a woman, please don't judge how worthwhile, needed, and loved you are by our inept ability to express our true feelings. Your divinely conferred trait of giving of self without counting the cost leads you to underestimate your own worth. (Richard G. Scott, "Plan of Happiness," 75.)

Your husband undoubtedly feels the same way about you.

Meeting the Emotional Needs of Your Husband

There is no more important duty for a wife than to be a partner and companion to her husband. Partnership implies an emotional bond that nurtures and supports. Companionship stirs images of walking hand-in-hand along the long and sometimes rocky path of life. Speaking of this aspect of marriage, President Gordon B. Hinckley stated: "Make of your marriage a partnership. . . . I am satisfied that God our Eternal Father does not love His daughters less than He loves His sons. Under the gospel plan the wife walks neither ahead nor behind her husband, but at his side in a true companionship before the Lord," ("Rise to the Stature," 97).

Although your husband may often appear to be confident and independent, know that he carries a substantial burden as he strives to provide for your family and be an effective father. Understanding the demands of your husband's job, the pressures he faces, the relationships he has with supervisors or bosses, and other stresses of his employment are a part of understanding your husband's emotional needs. Some men don't open up and share such matters easily; they often mask their true feelings. But you are your husband's chief therapist. Encourage him to share concerns about his work, his fears, his anxieties, and what you can do to assist him to square up his shoulders and carry off his side of the family enterprise.

At the end of a work day, he may need to come home to a much different situation than he faced in his job. Allow him the emotional space to wind down. Avoid the tendency to dump all your troubles on him the moment he comes through the door. When the time is more appropriate, encourage him to share his burdens. Don't settle for "Oh, nothing" or "Just the same old stuff." Gently tease it out of him. Reassure him that you appreciate his efforts to bless you and your children. Be his sounding board, one who will not necessarily try to solve every problem, but one who will listen and respond with ideas. Over time, he will feel progressively more safe in disclosing his fears and concerns and vulnerabilities because he knows you will not betray his trust, and he will be increasingly receptive to your ideas.

Take time to share with him what information has come to you about your children. He is gone much of the day and is often unaware of their feelings, activities, and needs. He wants to have an individual relationship with each of the children and he will be a better father when he knows what events have taken place in their lives.

Support any decisions that you prayerfully make together. Undoubtedly, he will counsel with you in the major decisions that affect you and your family; but once decisions are made, avoid the temptation to second-guess, criticize, or say, "I told you so." Be supportive of his efforts in his Church callings. It is a great comfort to him when he knows that you sustain him wholeheartedly.

Another thing that your husband probably needs and something that helps build emotional closeness between you is for you to be flexible. Men don't always plan as well as they should and they tend to be more spontaneous. He may, for example, get the idea while driving home from work that the family ought to go out to a movie or to a ballgame. Or he may plan a spur-of-the-moment getaway for a night or weekend. Respond positively to his invitations. If you are available for these kinds of activities, it will bless your marriage and help build a strong emotional bond between you.

MEETING THE PHYSICAL NEEDS OF YOUR HUSBAND

Your husband probably views sex quite differently than you do. Recognize that his desire for physical intimacy is a direct way for him to communicate to you his profound feelings of love, a therapeutic means of relieving stress when he is roughed up by the events and activities of life, and a way to experience intense feelings of pleasure and enjoyment with you. Recognize his need for diversity in your intimate relationship and don't wait for your husband to always initiate sexual activity. He will be thrilled if you will take the lead in intimate encounters from time to time.

In the previous chapter, we counseled husbands to exercise self-control when it is needed because you have many things to worry about besides being his sex partner. You may need periodic talks and frequent monitoring of your feelings about your desire for, and the proper frequency, of intimate contact. You need to explain to your husband when you are not feeling well, or when you are exhausted from life's duties. Husbands are generally understanding when they know that their wives would like to be intimate, but the timing is simply not good. "Perhaps we can try tomorrow," said by a wife is a better response than just plain old "No, I don't feel like it." Your husband is not a mind reader. Help him to understand your emotional state, but when you have made a promise for tomorrow, make good on it.

If you are not as easily aroused sexually as your husband is, teach him how to meet your needs. Tell him what is stimulating and enjoyable for you and how you like to proceed. Over time you will teach him to become the kind of sweetheart and lover you want him to be. You can best help with such phrases as, "You know what helps me the most?" Or, "What is really enjoyable for me is when you...." (You fill in the blanks.)

A common problem for a woman is "shifting gears." A man is able to leave work at the end of the day and come home to an emotional refuge. Of course, he may have church work or other responsibilities in the evening, but these things are usually not as stressful for him as his normal job. A woman, however, really never leaves her workplace. She always has things to do, and her work may not get done by the end of the day. Therefore, when it comes time for intimacy, she may still be preoccupied with her duties and be unable to shift gears from that of homemaker to that of lover. Addressing this problem, one woman explained what she does to help her: "I try to give myself permission to quit working at a designated hour, regardless of how much is left to finish. Sometimes I take a hot bath, listen to relaxing music, go for a walk, or do something else that helps me to unwind. This really helps me to prepare mentally to become my husband's sweetheart." Weekend getaways also allow a wife to leave daily responsibilities behind and focus more on her relationship with her husband. For most couples, this is very therapeutic for their relationship.

A word of caution: Do not use sex as a manipulative tool. Sex is not a reward or punishment for behavior. Don't withhold intimacy as a way to get even, to seek revenge, or to teach your husband a lesson. Let your interactions with him be a reflection of your deep feelings of respect and love. If you feel used and unappreciated, share that with him at a time when neither one of you is emotional. Gently teach him. Sometimes counseling may be needed to work through these kinds of feelings if they have been present for a long period of time.

If, in preparing for intimacy, you notice that your husband does not have an erection, kissing and embracing each other and gentle touching in his genital area will usually begin the process of sexual arousal for him. Normally, the more sexually aroused he becomes, the more sensitive the genital area becomes. But touching and handling your husband's penis is not going to injure it.

As you know from Chapter 4, once your husband has an erection, continued stimulation will usually bring him to orgasm without much difficulty. However, for intimacy to be enjoyable for you as a couple, you need to learn together to control the timing and amount of his stimulation so that you can both experience fulfillment. You may want him to help you experience orgasm before he does. If so, tell him. If he has reached a climax and you have not, teach him how to help you have the same experience.

TEACHING THROUGH SHAPING

We have talked about the importance of teaching each other in the marriage. We use the word "shaping" to indicate a way in which marriage partners become better teachers. The principle of shaping is one of expressing appreciation to your spouse when he acts as you would like (or comes close to your ideal). "Thanks for taking off your muddy shoes before coming in the house," usually results in him continuing the behavior.

Shaping has application to sexual relations as well. After a couple have been married for a period of time, they may skip the tender foreplay and romance they practiced earlier in marriage. Sometimes your husband may forget the importance of setting the proper emotional stage for you. You may need to shape your husband's sexual techniques. You might say to him, "You know what I loved about last night? We took our time. We weren't in a hurry. We both were relaxed and enjoyed each other. Sometimes I feel that we are so pressured to finish before the kids wake up or come home from their activities, that we don't really take time to enjoy being together. But, last night, it was so fun. We were not hurried, and it was very romantic for me. It was wonderful. Thanks."

In this example, positive feedback helps your husband realize that it is more romantic for you when you are not hurried. It is a way for you to gently and positively share your preferences with him. Of course, you can't have a candlelight dinner all the time with children around, but shaping is an effective way to help your spouse know what is on your wish list.

SUMMARY

Your husband has emotional, spiritual, and physical needs, just as you do. Your role as a wife is to help your husband fulfill those needs. Over the course of your marriage, your husband's desires, hopes, dreams, and aspirations will be revealed through your many discussions and exchanges. Although the stereotype is that men do not easily share their feelings, sensitive questioning and careful listening will help you determine what lies in the heart of your companion and enable you to know how to best help the man you love to be the kind of husband and father you would like him to be.

Sexual intimacy is an important aspect of your husband's relationship with you. For him, much of how he feels about you (and himself) is wrapped up in the spirit, emotions, and sensations of sexual contact. You may not necessarily understand why sex is so important to him, and your perspective may be different, but put yourself in his place occasionally and try to appreciate his nature and needs just as he must do with you. If you can, you will better understand him and be able to meet his needs, sexual and otherwise. In doing so, you can create a union that is mutually fulfilling, uplifting, and a joy to you both.

CHAPTER 15

Drawing the Line

A question frequently asked by young men and women of dating age is: "How far can we go in expressing our affection without crossing the line?" Parents and youth leaders respond with principles and stories to illustrate the point that any sexual activity before marriage is off-limits and out-of-bounds. Elder Richard G. Scott said it best: "Any sexual intimacy outside of the bonds of marriage—I mean any intentional contact with the sacred, private parts of another's body, with or without clothing—is a sin and is forbidden by God. It is also a transgression to intentionally stimulate these emotions within your own body," (*Ensign*, November 1994:38). The message is clear: our young people should exercise self-control and live by the spirit of the Law of Chastity.

Interestingly, one of the questions most frequently asked by married couples is the same as their unmarried counterparts: "How far can we go in expressing our love without crossing the line of propriety?" Some couples assume that, because they are married, any type of sexual behavior between the two of them is acceptable. Does marriage allow unrestricted sexual activity?

GOSPEL INSIGHTS

The Lord said, "Come . . . and let us reason together, that ye may understand," (D&C 50:10). We all need to consider this matter as married couples. President Boyd K. Packer commented on his concern:

> With ever fewer exceptions, [the things] we see and read and hear have the mating act as a central theme. Censorship is forced offstage as a violation of individual freedom. That which should be absolutely private is disrobed and acted out center stage. In the shadows, backstage are addiction, pornography, perversion, infidelity, abortion, incest, and molestation. In company with them now is a plague of biblical proportion. And all of them are on the increase. Society excuses itself from responsibility except for teaching the physical process of reproduction to children in school to prevent pregnancy and disease and providing teenagers with devices which are supposed to protect them from both. When any effort is made to include values in these courses—basic universal values, not just values of the Church, but of civilization, of society itself—the protest arises, "You are imposing religion upon us, infringing upon our freedom." (*Ensign,* May 1992:66.)

The sexual "looseness" of our day has allowed many to introduce their ideas about sexual behavior into the popular media discourse so that what was once shunned as base and vulgar is now considered a necessary topic for public discussion. Any effort to criticize, or to insist on decency and restraint is labeled "censorship." President Gordon B. Hinckley expressed his disappointment with the explicitness of our day:

> Never before, at least not in our generation, have the forces of evil been so blatant, so brazen, so aggressive as they are today. Things we dared not speak about in earlier times are now constantly projected into our living rooms. All sensitivity is cast aside as reporters and pundits speak with a disgusting plainness of things that can only stir curiosity and lead to evil. (*Ensign,* November 1998:102.)

In his remarks to the women of the Church, President Hinckley challenged them to do something about this problem: "If anyone can change the dismal situation into which we are sliding, it is you. Rise up, O women of Zion, rise to the great challenge which faces you. Stand above the sleaze and the filth and the temptation which is all about you," (Ibid., 98–99).

Pornography has made major inroads into our society. Unprecedented filth is available from every corner video store, cable and network television, the Internet, and cinema. Like a flood, this material seems to be overwhelming our culture. What was once considered filthy and kept in the back alley now comes into our homes in living color. Avoiding pornography has been a constant theme of Church leaders in the last two decades. President Hinckley has been most forthright:

> This stuff is titillating, it is attractive, it is made so. Leave it alone! Get away from it! Avoid it! It is sleazy filth! It is rot that will do no good! You cannot afford to watch video tapes of this kind of stuff. You cannot afford to read magazines that are designed to destroy you. You can't do it, nor even watch it on television. . . . Stay away from it! Avoid it like the plague because it is just as deadly, more so. The plague will destroy the body. Pornography will destroy the body and the soul. Stay away from it! It is as a great disease that is sweeping over the country and over the entire world. Avoid it! I repeat, avoid it! Avoid it! (*Church News*, 1997:2.)

On another occasion, he cautioned:

> Be careful of what you read. . . . Avoid the foul language, the titillating rubbish of many TV programs, of videotapes, of sensual magazines, of 900-numbers, and the filth that I am told is now found on the Internet. These will bring you no benefit, and they could destroy you. (*Ensign*, March 1997:62.)

RESTRAINT

While the world has been madly pursuing ever more blatant displays of sexual behavior, prophets and apostles have sounded ominous warnings. Church leaders have plainly taught that marriage does not give license to deviancy or the introduction of unholy sexual practices into marriage. President Kimball said that, "even in marriage there can be some excesses and distortions. No amount of rationalization to the contrary can satisfy a disappointed Father in Heaven," (*Ensign*, May 1974:7).

President Ezra Taft Benson, as president of the Twelve, quoted President Kimball and gave this counsel:

> The world would have you accept a so-called new morality, which is nothing more than immorality. Our living prophet has reaffirmed that the eternal standard of chastity has not changed. Here are his words: "The world may have its norm; the Church has a different one. . . . The world may countenance premarital sex experiences, but the Lord and His church condemn in no uncertain terms any and every sex relationship outside of marriage, and even indecent and uncontrolled ones within marriage. And so, though many self-styled authorities justify these practices as a normal release, the Church condemns them. . . . Such unholy practices were condemned by ancient prophets and are today condemned by the Church." This standard means keeping yourselves clean in body and mind. The Church has no double standard of morality. The moral code of heaven for both men and women is complete chastity before marriage and full fidelity after marriage. (*Ensign*, November 1977:31.)

In 1978, President N. Eldon Tanner, of the First Presidency, in a General Priesthood meeting, expressed his concerns to a body of priesthood members:

> Brethren, we who lead the Church are responsible to see that you are taught in plainness. I, therefore, must make reference to a matter that otherwise I would not present in a meeting such as this. There are evil and degrading practices which, in the world, are not only condoned but encouraged. Sometimes married couples in

their intimate expression of love to one another are drawn into practices that are unholy, unworthy, and unnatural. We receive letters from time to time asking for a definition of "unnatural" or "unworthy." Brethren, you know the answer to that. If in doubt at all, do not do it. Surely no holder of the priesthood would feel worthy to accept advancement in the priesthood or sign his temple recommend if any impure practice were a part of his life. If perchance, one of you has been drawn into any degrading conduct, cast it away from you so that when you are subject to a worthiness interview you can answer to yourself, and to the Lord, and to the interviewing priesthood officer that you are worthy. (*Ensign*, November 1978:42.)

COERCION

Gospel covenants are between an individual and God, and the covenant of marriage is no exception. When a man and a woman enter into the marriage covenant, they become accountable to their Father in Heaven for the way in which they carry out those holy promises. This accountability extends to how they treat each other in all phases of their lives, including their intimate relationship. Unfortunately, Church leaders hear accounts of spouses being "forced" or "coerced" into forms of sexual conduct repulsive to them. Often those offended want to know if they have to participate in specific sexual acts to keep a spouse happy and the marriage intact. In 1990, President Gordon B. Hinckley reflected on some personal correspondence:

> I have in my office a file of letters received from women who cry out over the treatment they receive from their husbands in their homes. They tell of the activity of some of these men in Church responsibilities. They even speak of men holding temple recommends. And they speak of abuse, both subtle and open. They tell of husbands who lose their tempers and shout at their wives and children. They tell of men who demand offensive intimate relations. (*Ensign*, May 1990:52.)

Clearly, coercion of any kind is offensive and inappropriate, and cannot be considered acceptable in marriage. Coercion is a form of abuse. It is a form of unrighteous dominion (D&C 121:39). Prophets have consistently counseled that marriage does not give a spouse permission to exploit their companion for personal gratification in the name of conjugal rights or duties. If one person insists on a behavior that offends his or her spouse or makes a particular act a test of the spouse's marital love, the line of good sense and propriety has obviously been crossed. In his address to the general priesthood of the Church, President Howard W. Hunter, counseled men:

> Keep yourselves above any domineering or unworthy behavior in the tender, intimate relationship between husband and wife. Because marriage is ordained of God, the intimate relationship between husbands and wives is good and honorable in the eyes of God. He has commanded that they be one flesh and that they multiply and replenish the earth (Moses 2:28; 3:24). You are to love your wife as Christ loved the Church and gave himself for it (Ephesians 5:25–31). Tenderness and respect—never selfishness—must be the guiding principles in the intimate relationship between husband and wife. Each partner must be considerate and sensitive to the other's needs and desires. *Any domineering, indecent, or uncontrolled behavior in the intimate relationship between husband and wife is condemned by the Lord. Any man who abuses or demeans his wife physically or spiritually is guilty of grievous sin and in need of sincere and serious repentance.* Differences should be worked out in love and kindness and with a spirit of mutual reconciliation. A man should always speak to his wife lovingly and kindly, treating her with the utmost respect. Marriage is like a tender flower, brethren, and must be nourished constantly with expressions of love and affection. (*Ensign*, Nov. 1994:51, emphasis added.)

UNNATURAL BEHAVIOR

In addition to behavior that is forced by one spouse upon another, we have also been counseled against acts that have been labeled "unnatural" and "unholy" and that constitute an offense to the Spirit. While not giving specific details as to what behaviors are excessive and inappropriate, President Kimball on one occasion gave this counsel:

> If it is unnatural, you just don't do it. That is all, and all the family life should be kept clean and worthy and on a very high plane. There are some people who have said that behind the bedroom doors anything goes. That is not true and the Lord would not condone it. (Kimball, *Teachings*, 312.)

Church leaders are concerned about being too explicit in their remarks and thereby stirring curiosity. They don't attempt to define terms; rather, they teach and reason about general principles, hoping that Church members will have ears to hear without the need for specific or detailed explanations and proscriptions. In an address at Brigham Young University, President Boyd K. Packer talked about propriety in marital relations:

> I must include a caution to you who are married. A couple may be tempted to introduce things into [their] relationship which are unworthy. Do not, as the scriptures warn, "change the natural use into that which is against nature," (Rom. 1:26). If you do, the tempter will drive a wedge between you. If something unworthy has become part of your relationship, don't ever do it again! Now, what exactly do I mean by that? You know what I mean by that. (Packer, "Fountain of Life," 8.)

The message repeatedly stressed by Church leaders is that there is a line to be drawn between that which is uplifting, enriching, and unifying, and that which is degrading, unholy, and destructive. However, given every couple's unique combination of physical and psychological responses and needs, it is difficult to suggest clear statements about what is appropriate or inappropriate for a particular couple. However, we do not hesitate to say that unnatural sexual relations, by common sense and reason, should be off-limits for any Latter-day Saint couple.

Elder Boyd K. Packer indicated in a Brigham Young University devotional, "We do not, in our counseling, enter the bedrooms of members of the Church," (Packer, "The Fountain of Life," 8). Since each couple is unique, and since adequate sexual arousal is difficult for many individuals, there is an apparent distinction between fore-play—those preparatory arousal techniques that make sexual inter-course possible and enjoyable—and intercourse itself. What a couple does to bring each other to a state of arousal sufficient to complete the sexual experience is left (within appropriate bounds) to the discre-tion of the couple.

When our love for each other is centered in wholesome sexual practices, and charity serves as the ruling virtue in our effort to bless one another, we are free to learn from each other what is pleasing and essential for satisfying spousal sexual relations. There are proper ways to arouse sexual passion, but, as we have stressed repeatedly, an under-standing of what is appropriate and fulfilling is best learned from one's spouse, as each endeavors to be sensitive to the whisperings of the Spirit. How can husbands and wives determine propriety in these sensitive matters? They can do it in the same way they determine the correctness of any course of action, by taking the issue to the Lord in a spirit of humility, faith, and prayer. In this manner, every couple can discern what is wholesome and enriching to their marriage, and what is potentially degrading and destructive. We encourage creativity, variety, adventure, and playfulness on the part of both married part-ners. In a spirit of love and tenderness, and by giving gentle teaching and feedback, couples can create an environment of affection that is both in harmony with gospel teachings and ennobling to the marriage.

Summary

The Lord designed marital intimacy to be an integral part of marriage, an expression of tenderness and care. God himself commands this union. But sex is a stewardship properly reserved for those who enter the covenants of marriage. Such a stewardship requires that passions be checked and channeled in order to nurture physical and spiritual fulfillment within the bounds set by a loving Creator. Any sexual behavior that offends a spouse or distances a couple from the Spirit of the Lord is a violation of the sacred steward-ship we have received.

CHAPTER 16

Twenty Questions

QUESTION 1: *How important is the sexual part of the married relationship to most people? What is a normal frequency of sexual relations?*

ANSWER: Sexual intimacy is an important part of married life for most couples. However, there are some who do not particularly enjoy this aspect of their relationship or who do not need sexual intimacy very often. But this is clearly not the norm, especially among younger couples. The vast majority of husbands and wives want and need the closeness that comes from sexual activity with each other on a regular basis.

The average frequency of sexual relations is dependent upon age. Some have said that when you're thirty it's "triweekly," at fifty it's "try weekly," and at seventy it's "try weakly!" In truth, the average is about two to three times per week among younger couples and two to six times per month among older couples. There is no correct amount, however. It depends entirely upon what each couple desires and needs.

QUESTION 2: *What is the clitoris? How important is it to sexual fulfillment?*

ANSWER: The clitoris is a female genital structure that is located about one inch above the urethra at the convergence of the two labia minora. It is partially covered at the top by a rim of tissue called the clitoral hood. In the embryo, the clitoris is made of the same tissue that makes up the penis in a male. It has no function other than to provide pleasure during sexual intimacy.

For most women, once they are adequately aroused, stimulation of the clitoris is the primary means of achieving orgasm. However, the clitoris does not usually receive direct stimulation during sexual intercourse. Indirect stimulation of the clitoris may occur as the labia minora stretch, placing pressure on the clitoris through the clitoral hood. However, this indirect stimulation may be insufficient for orgasm to occur. Additional direct stimulation of the clitoris may be required for this to happen. Ideally, the wife teaches the husband what her particular needs are and how to provide the proper kind of stimulation that allows her to experience orgasm.

Every woman differs in the character and timing of stimulation needed to reach orgasm. Light touching, perhaps assisted by a lubricant, is usually more effective than hard rubbing. Part of foreplay and the sexual adventure of marriage involves an exploration of what each spouse likes and needs. The wife must be willing to communicate what she needs, and the husband must be patient and sensitive enough to meet those needs.

QUESTION 3: *My husband isn't very sensitive to my needs. I'm not sure he even knows I'm there when we are together sexually. He is very mechanical in his approach. It's like he has a routine, and when it's over, it's over. What can I do?*

ANSWER: This is a common complaint. Fortunately, wives in the "younger" generation seem to indicate that it is less a problem than in the past. Your husband's insensitivity may be due to his background, his personality, or simple ignorance. Whatever the reason, you need to be the agent of change. Ultimately, if changes aren't made, you will probably not have a very satisfying intimate life together.

You need to have a frank discussion together about your concerns. Reassure him of your love, and of your confidence in him as a person. But make it clear that you desire more from your intimate times together. Share your sexual script with him—what you would like if you could make all the decisions. Explain exactly what you want, but be tactful, and take care to avoid hurt feelings and resistance. Men are inclined to feel threatened and defensive if criticized, so teach through experience that sex will be better for him if it's more enjoyable for you. Take the initiative to show him what is possible, and be willing to understand and respond to his sexual script as well. If you work at it constructively, sensitively, and lovingly, things will improve, and you will both be happier as a result.

Finally, if you don't think you can say what's on your mind, put your thoughts in writing, or hand him this book and have him read this question and answer.

QUESTION 4: *My wife's contraceptive diaphragm gets in the way of our intimate relations. What can we do?*

ANSWER: There are many birth control alternatives available to couples today. They are of varying effectiveness and each possesses a different set of side effects. Couples are encouraged to obtain advice from a medical professional in deciding what might best suit their needs, taking into consideration the health of the wife, and the costs, risks, and effectiveness of each method.

Most young women today choose hormonal forms of contraception. This is because these birth control methods are the most effective and the simplest to use. Four basic options are available: the standard combination birth control pill, the mini-pill, contraceptive injections, and contraceptive subcutaneous implants. The two most popular methods are the combination pill and contraceptive injections. This is because the mini-pill is associated with higher failure rates and unacceptable side effects and implants are expensive and designed to last for five years. Engaged couples should be aware that hormonal birth control needs to be initiated at least four to six weeks prior to the wedding. Starting it this early also allows for some adjustment of the timing of the woman's menstrual period so that she is not menstruating on her wedding day.

Barrier forms of contraception include the contraceptive diaphragm and condoms. These may not be the best choices for newlywed couples. A diaphragm can be difficult to use, and condoms detract from the spontaneity and enjoyment of the sexual experience for many couples.

The intrauterine device (IUD) is again available for use after having been removed from the market for a brief period of time in the 1980s. When used in proper situations, it is a safe and reliable form of contraception. The IUD is not recommended for women who have not had children, however, because it is still associated with an increased incidence of pelvic infection which, in some cases, can result in infertility or future tubal pregnancy.

Other forms of birth control, such as contraceptive suppositories and foams, have such high failure rates that they cannot be recommended unless there are reasons why all other forms of contraception cannot be used.

QUESTION 5: *My wife is very reluctant to talk about our sexual relationship. We have problems that I feel we need to discuss. When I bring up my concerns she refuses to talk about them. What can I do?*

ANSWER: It is essential that couples communicate about marital intimacy. But most marriages are made up of ordinary people with normal, and sometimes inadequate, communication skills. Fortunately, in the Church, many young people serve missions or have roommates prior to marriage. These are great experiences for learning communication skills. Even those experiences, however, don't completely prepare someone for living with another person for the rest of their life. Even the best prepared spouse will need to continue developing communication skills.

One has to wonder why your wife is so reluctant to discuss sexual matters. Is she afraid of being criticized or ridiculed? Sometimes marriage partners have difficulty opening up on a given subject because they have been hurt when doing so in the past. Be sure you're not belittling her when she tries to initiate a conversation or respond to your questions. Treat her concerns with dignity and respect.

There are a number of ways you can encourage her to communicate better. A variety of seminars are available for helping husbands and wives learn to express their thoughts clearly and listen properly. Self-help texts are also available on this subject. These can teach both of you how to better express your concerns in a nonthreatening and constructive manner. Using emotionally neutral statements like "I am concerned about our sexual interaction because . . ." are much better than the inflammatory ones such as "I don't like it when you . . ."

Marriage counselors are particularly good at getting married couples to talk to each other. A few visits to one will pay great dividends for you. As impartial third parties, they can help overcome problems or resolve impasses that may be present in your marriage. Counseling is usually much more effective before a crisis develops, so don't wait until the marriage is at the breaking point.

QUESTION 6: *How do I know whether I am ready to have sex? I can't even use tampons yet.*

ANSWER: We strongly recommend that all young women have a physical examination by a medical professional prior to marriage. There are some anatomic conditions that prevent consummation of sexual union that can be corrected by a physician. If, by about age eighteen, a young woman has tried to use a tampon and has not been able to insert it successfully, she should have a pelvic examination.

QUESTION 7: *We have been married for two years. My wife still talks about her old boyfriend and she calls him from time to time. This bothers me a lot. I feel like I don't have her complete commitment, and it affects my ability to perform sexually with her. What can I do?*

ANSWER: The Apostle Paul said that when we grow up we should leave childish things behind us (1 Corinthians 13:11). An old romance is a thing of the past. It is something that is getting in the way of your personal and marital progress. So, yes, your wife should not continue her relationship with her old boyfriend. She needs to stop talking about him and calling him, especially since she knows it bothers you.

That is not the only question for you, however. You need to honestly consider why you are so bothered by this old boyfriend. How secure are you in the relationship? Could it be a control issue for you? Does she do it because she feels smothered by you? Are there other issues involved? As a couple, you need to take a close look at the dynamics of your relationship. If she stops calling her old boyfriend and you still have performance difficulties that can't be resolved on your own, you should probably see a counselor or a physician.

QUESTION 8: *I've heard about Kegel's exercises. What are they and what do they do?*

ANSWER: Arnold Kegel was a gynecologist in the 1940s who discovered that exercises of the muscles of the pelvic floor in women resulted in improvement of a certain kind of urinary incontinence. The exercises involve contraction and relaxation of the muscle that helps support the vagina, bladder, and urethra. Women can voluntarily contract this muscle if they tighten up the same muscle they use to stop the flow of urine.

Kegel's exercises can result in increased tone of the vaginal canal, and therefore, increase enjoyment of sexual intercourse for some women. This seems to be particularly true for women who, as a result of childbearing, have relaxation of the vaginal canal.

When doing Kegel's exercises, a woman should contract the pelvic floor muscles five to ten times, holding each contraction for ten seconds. This sequence should be repeated three or four times per day. Results will usually not be noticed until after several months of exercise, and, unfortunately, some women do not see any improvement from these exercises.

QUESTION 9: *I have absolutely no interest in having sex. In fact, the thought of it makes me sick. What can I do?*

ANSWER: You have a potentially serious problem. You probably have what is known as Sexual Aversion Disorder. People with this condition, most of whom are women, often have a deep-seated psychological basis for their problem. Sexual situations engender disgust, fear, anger, revulsion, or anxiety. Some individuals may become physically sick when faced with physical intimacy, even in marriage.

Most individuals with sexual aversion have had traumatic experiences—usually of a sexual nature—in the past. These experiences may include molestation, rape, or incest, but they may also involve other emotional insults that have been transferred subconsciously to a sexual context. You need to obtain counseling from someone who is skilled in handling this kind of problem. Contact the medical school closest to you and ask for a clinic that deals with sexual dysfunction. You could also call your gynecologist for a referral. It is an easy call to make, and can improve your marital relationship in dramatic ways. If you don't get help, sex will very likely be a significant problem in your marriage.

QUESTION 10: *I think my husband is sex-crazed. He wants sex all of the time. I've told him that I don't feel the same way he does. This makes him mad, and he pouts when I say "no." What can be done?*

ANSWER: A difference in sexual desire between young spouses is the number one sexual problem in early marriage. Very early in the marriage it usually isn't an issue, but once you move out of the "honeymoon" phase, it can be a major problem when one spouse doesn't feel the same level of sexual interest as the other.

You didn't say how often he wants to have sexual relations. If it's daily or less, then that's not uncommon. If he insists on sex several times a day, then he may, indeed, have a problem. In the latter case, one has to wonder why he wants sexual intimacy so often. From a psychiatric perspective, several conditions need to be ruled out, including bipolar disorder, obsessive-compulsive disorder, borderline personality disorder, and addictive behavior. Medical conditions such as endocrine and neurologic problems also need to be considered.

If your husband is psychologically and medically stable, the next step is to evaluate how he responds to your denials for sex. Is he willing to compromise? Is he willing to rationally discuss the issue? When he is rebuffed, does he become depressed, unable to function, or retaliatory? If so, counseling should be sought, because this is abnormal behavior for mature adults.

Finally, it may be that you just have different sexual natures. Not everyone's libido is the same. If this is the case, you need to have a good discussion about it, or both of you will be unhappy with your constant sexual tug-of-war. Talk about it until you are both happy with where your sexual relationship stands, and keep the communication lines open.

QUESTION 11: *I'm getting married in about four months. However, I want to be a virgin when we get married, so I don't want to have a pelvic exam beforehand. Is this OK?*

ANSWER: For some reason, there are individuals who think that if they undergo a pelvic exam, they will lose their virginity. Please understand that this is not the case. Having a pelvic exam or inserting a tampon does not render a woman unchaste. Chastity before marriage requires abstaining from all sexual relations, but this has nothing to do with medical procedures such as examinations or surgery.

Premarital exams are extremely useful. They can help discover conditions that could make it difficult for you to have sex. It will also give you a chance to talk about birth control or ask any questions you may have about sexuality and reproduction. Be assured that you'll be better informed and no less a virgin when you walk out of the doctor's office than when you walked in.

QUESTION 12: *I have PMS. When I have it, I don't want anyone near me. I don't want my husband around, especially not for sex. It really affects our relationship a lot. The rest of the time we get along very well. Why do I feel this way; and what can I do?*

ANSWER: PMS is an abbreviation for Premenstrual Syndrome. It is a collection of physical, emotional, and behavioral symptoms that some women experience on a cyclic basis before their menstrual period begins. The cause of PMS has never been discovered, although there are many theories.

Perhaps as many as seventy-five percent of women have some discomfort or irritability in the premenstrual phase. However, from a medical point of view, a few minor premenstrual symptoms do not constitute PMS. The diagnosis of Premenstrual Syndrome is reserved for women whose symptoms significantly affect their ability to function normally. About ten to fifteen percent of women are thought to have true PMS.

The diagnosis of PMS should not be made lightly since other medical and psychological problems mimic it. Psychological problems such as depression, seasonal affective disorder, borderline personality disorders, and anxiety must be considered. Thyroid disease, diabetes, and autoimmune problems, among others, also need to be ruled out.

The hallmark of PMS is that the symptoms are triggered by ovulation and recede with menstruation. Typically, PMS symptoms start within a week of the onset of the menstrual period and end soon after the period begins. PMS virtually never occurs in the period between menstruation and the next ovulation. If symptoms are noticed during this time frame, other medical or psychological problems should be suspected.

The physical symptoms of PMS include fatigue, headache, bloating, breast tenderness, insomnia, and fluid retention. Emotional symptoms include depression, anxiety, hostility, irritability, mood swings, sensitivity to rejection, and decreased sex drive. Behavioral changes include food cravings (including chocolate, sugar, and alcohol), binge eating, intolerance of alcohol, and abuse of others. The symptoms seem to worsen between age thirty and menopause, both in severity of symptoms and the number of days that PMS is present each month.

Many treatments for PMS have been promoted with varying success. Most treatments include exercise, vitamins, and other nutritional supplements. Avoiding sugar, refined flour, caffeine, carbonated beverages, red meat, and whole milk products helps many women. Increased intake of fruits, vegetables, poultry, fish, and low-fat dairy products and calcium also may help. Medications that treat specific symptoms are occasionally helpful, including diuretics and anti-anxiety medications. Progesterone was once thought to be a cure for PMS, but objective studies have not proven its value, although it does seem to help some women.

Over the past decade, a number of studies have demonstrated the benefit of drugs that alter the brain chemistry of serotonin and epinephrine. This family of drugs, collectively known as serotonin-reuptake inhibitors, has been found to significantly reduce the symptoms associated with PMS. Many women notice near-complete resolution of their symptoms with these medications.

You should consult a doctor about your condition. If it is decided that you have PMS, you can then talk about treatment possibilities.

QUESTION 13: *Our son is getting married in a few months. In thinking about his upcoming wedding, we began to reflect upon our wedding night. When we went on our honeymoon, we were both totally exhausted from the days' events, which included a lot a travel to the wedding and the reception. Our first sexual experience was very difficult, primarily because we were so tired. Any ideas on what we can recommend to our son so he and his new wife don't have the same experience?*

ANSWER: It is important that the honeymoon go smoothly. But it is more important to keep things in perspective. The wedding night is just one night. So don't let preparations for the wedding, or the honeymoon, overshadow the couple's need to focus on being prepared spiritually and emotionally for marriage. Similarly, the wedding must take precedence over the festivities that accompany it. The couple's deepest attention should be given to the sacred blessings bestowed in the ceremony.

Once that is carefully addressed, you can move on to concerns about the honeymoon. If possible, create a situation where the bride and the groom are not exhausted when they check into the hotel. Their first experience with intimacy is important, and proper preparation can bless the marriage immediately and in the days and years that follow.

Why not try to remove everything from the wedding day that could be a distraction from the sacred nature of the occasion? Of course, when family and friends travel long distances for the wedding, it may be necessary to have the reception or open house on the same day. But consider having the reception the night before the wedding or after the honeymoon. Then the wedding day can consist of a morning or early afternoon wedding, pictures, and a bite to eat. Then, the couple can be on their way at a reasonable hour.

QUESTION 14: *My wife and I are infertile. We have been attempting to get pregnant for two years and are undergoing fertility treatments. The stress of not getting pregnant has caused some sexual problems, since we must have intercourse on a specific schedule. Sometimes I have difficulty under these circumstances. It seems like I'm just there as the donor with a job to do. Much of the joy of sex is now gone, since it's more a chore than a pleasure. My wife feels the same way. Any ideas to help?*

ANSWER: Infertile couples often report these problems. Having intercourse on a scheduled basis is not enjoyable for most people since the spontaneity of the experience is lost. Men frequently report situational impotence under these conditions. Women may also notice little arousal or enjoyment since they're so worried about whether they are doing everything right.

Individuals in infertile relationships may feel guilt, sadness, or anger over their inability to have a child. They may also feel a sense of failure as a man or women. The angst engendered by infertility can be emotionally transferred to the sexual experience itself. When this happens, sex becomes a source of guilt, sadness, or anger, or a reminder of their failure. Some couples may even stop having sexual activity except when it is absolutely required to avoid negative feelings.

Most doctors who deal with infertility are aware of these potential problems and warn their patients about them. Talk to your wife's specialist about what is going on. He or she should be able to give you some direction on the matter. Also, it is not necessary for a couple to have intercourse every night in order to conceive, even when there is an infertility problem. Every two to three nights around the time of ovulation is satisfactory in most cases.

Think of ways to make the "required" sex less of a chore. Find the fun again. Go on a date beforehand. Look for a romantic new location. Don't worry too much about what day of the cycle your wife is on or waste your attention wondering whether this will be the night she gets pregnant. In other words, if you can, focus less on the reproductive aspect of sex and more on its other dimensions.

After doing these things, if sexual problems persist, you should probably consider some counseling. Getting help from a counselor can allow you to overcome your problems and keep your marriage strong in the face of the frequently daunting process of infertility treatment.

QUESTION 15: *Since the delivery of my fourth child I have developed a new problem. When we have sex it feels fine until I have an orgasm, but when I experience climax I have very severe pain. Is this normal?*

ANSWER: This is somewhat uncommon. The pain may be due to varicose veins in the pelvic area. As you know, varicose veins can occur in the legs as a result of pregnancy. These usually get worse with each succeeding pregnancy. Varicose veins can also occur in the vessels surrounding the uterus. When sexual arousal occurs, the pelvic veins swell with blood through vasocongestion. If the veins are already abnormally large, they can dilate to such an extent during orgasm that pain occurs, just as varicosities in the legs get painful when they swell from standing too long. Pelvic varicosities can also cause an increase in premenstrual and menstrual pain, since the veins are more dilated at these times of the cycle. Some doctors call this Pelvic

Congestion Syndrome. Of course, this diagnosis needs to be confirmed by your gynecologist, who can review other possible causes of pelvic pain.

QUESTION 16: *My wife has stretch marks on her stomach from her pregnancy. They really turn me off. I don't have the same interest in her I once had. She complains that I ignore her, and we don't have sex very often now. What do you suggest?*

ANSWER: This is your problem—not your wife's—and you need to resolve it. Every man and woman has sexual cues to which he or she responds. Your wife's stretch marks bother you, but it's something you have to work through. We don't live in a constant world. We will not always look like we did on our wedding day. We change. You need to accept the fact that your wife is no longer just your wife and lover. She is now a mother, and she has paid a physical price in giving you a child and making you a father. She didn't ask for the stretch marks; she's undoubtedly as distressed by them as you are. If it helps, take solace in the fact that in time the stretch marks will fade; but that won't matter much if your love has also faded by then. Give her a break now, and show some charity and understanding. If you take a look in the mirror, you'll probably discover you aren't what you used to be either. And you can always turn out the lights if it will help.

QUESTION 17: *For the past week, it hurts when I urinate or ejaculate. It scares me. What could be the problem?*

ANSWER: You most likely have cystitis or urethritis. Cystitis is a bacterial infection of the bladder. Urethritis is an infection of the urethra that is caused by bacteria, mycoplasma, or chlamydia. You might even have an infection of the epididymus or prostate gland. All of these infections are treatable, and depending upon the kind of infection you have, your wife also may need to be treated. You should see a physician immediately.

QUESTION 18: *I am getting married soon. I will be a virgin when we get married. However, I want things to be good for us sexually. I want to be able to enjoy it without any problems. How can I know whether or not we'll experience problems in our sex life?*

ANSWER: You are to be applauded for your determination to be sexually pure at the time of your wedding. It will be a source of great joy throughout your marriage for each of you to know that you have never shared yourself sexually with anyone else. Perhaps the best advice for the honeymoon is to relax and enjoy one another without worrying about how well you perform. You are beginners, and there will be plenty of time over the upcoming years to get things right.

The fulfillment you find in marital intimacy is up to the two of you. Being a virgin does not ensure that everything will run smoothly in the area of sexual intimacy. Potential problems lurk at the fringes of all marriage relationships. You will face emotional, spiritual, and physical challenges over the next sixty or so years of marriage. Things will not always be uncomplicated. But if you are loving, patient, communicative, humble, and teachable, you will have a wonderful adventure together in the long run. These qualities will help you work through any problems that may arise.

QUESTION 19: *My husband gives me no warning at all. I'm up to my elbows in dishes and laundry after the kids are asleep. He's only got one thing on his mind—he wants me in the bedroom. Why is he so insensitive?*

ANSWER: He may not be as insensitive as he is ignorant. Men think differently than women. Perhaps he needs to learn that the way to your heart is through the soapsuds on his elbows. Some guys are slower than others, so give him some help. Teach him how you think and how you feel. Tell him that your reluctance to hop into bed the minute the kids are asleep has little to do with your love for him, and a lot to do with what's still in the kitchen sink. Tell him that it's important for you to have some sense of order in the house before you can get enthused about sex. And then show him that when he contributes around the house, you find him a lot more exciting. If you can discuss it together, he might even offer to take care of both the laundry and dishes later—while you get needed rest—if you'll drop everything and be with him right now.

QUESTION 20: *Should I buy a sex manual so I know what to do when we get married?*

ANSWER: Every couple benefits from education on sexual matters. Some books in the self-help section of the bookstore are well-written, balanced, and informative. However, there is much information, in both books and videos, that can have a negative effect. It can lead to improper experimentation, impure thoughts, and unrealistic expectations. One of the purposes of this book is to provide a reference that appropriately introduces the topic of human sexuality within a gospel framework. We have tried to dispense enough information to address the needs of married couples without slipping into telestial portrayals of sexual intimacy. We encourage young couples to be armed with basic information and then learn what they don't know from their spouse in a process of exploration and discovery that is truly rewarding.

Epilogue

In this book, we have discussed the importance and place of sexual relations in marriage. We began with a review of the central role of marriage and sexual intimacy in the Lord's Plan of Happiness. We outlined the basic principles upon which a successful intimate life is established, including a knowledge of the human sexual response as well as the gospel ideals that create an environment in marriage where sexual interaction can flourish properly. The differences between husbands and wives, and possible reasons for those differences, were explored. We reviewed aspects of sexual dysfunction and pointed out problems that are particularly prevalent at different stages of married life. Finally, specific advice was given to husbands and wives to enable both partners to better understand each other and help each achieve sexual fulfillment. Hopefully, readers have gained insights that will help them in the intimate aspects of marriage.

The topic of sexual intimacy enjoys a peculiar place in our society. Despite the high interest in the subject, for cultural and religious reasons, sexual issues are often not discussed openly or candidly between marriage partners. Consequently, when couples have problems, as most do at one time or another, they are hesitant to talk about them or to seek help. But clear and honest communication plays a vital role in a couple's intimacy. A husband and wife must listen to each other and teach one another to find fulfillment in their sexual relations.

Many parents also feel reluctant to talk to their children about sex—even older children who are preparing for marriage—either because they are embarrassed about the subject or because they are unsure of what to say or how to say it. One young married man shared this story:

> *My marriage day was the happiest time of my life. On our wedding day, I remember sitting in the celestial room with my wife and feeling such an overwhelming feeling of peace and joy. Everything was perfect. I remember feeling so happy until the reception ended. Then my feelings of joy turned to feelings of nervousness.*
>
> *The first reason for my nervousness came from the way I was brought up. Without intending to, my parents raised me to believe that sex was a sin. They focused way too much on moral transgression. I subconsciously believed that sex was dirty and wrong. As I grew older, I understood that in marriage it is okay, but my parents and people in the Church always focused on sexual sins and not enough on the good things that can come about through a healthy sexual relationship within the bonds of marriage. I thought sex was purely physical and had no connection to the spiritual and emotional well-being of both partners.*
>
> *The second reason I had difficulty in our sexual relationship was because of the influence of society on the way I viewed sex and sexual satisfaction. Since my parents did not talk with me very much about sex, I was left to figure it out on my own. Unfortunately, most of what I found out was from people who didn't know much about proper sexual relations and they got it from the television and movies. I got a lot of very differing ideas on what sex was from kids in junior high. In high school, I overhead stories from some Marines. These were not the proper sources to explain to me how Heavenly Father viewed sexual relations. Many of the ideas disgusted me and were purely based on self-pleasure. Nothing was said about making a partner happy or being concerned with their feelings about sex. Parents need not be unnecessarily explicit in explaining*

the sex act to their children, but they should definitely clear up the misconceptions that we learn in junior high and high school.

A young woman related a similar story:

I grew up in a family where it was a rarity that we talked about sex. When we did, it was usually in a family home evening type setting where I think my parents felt more at ease in addressing the issue of intimacy. When sex was discussed, my parents usually talked about how it was wrong to be sexually involved before marriage. Rarely did they address the fact that in marriage, sexual intimacy is a meaningful and beautiful facet to the marital relationship. Unfortunately, my Young Women teachers never approached intimacy with the right attitude, either. I think I was cheated as a result of being instilled with negative notions about sex. I admit that I was afraid before marriage of being sexually intimate with my future husband.

When I became engaged, I admitted to my future husband my fear of the idea of sexual intimacy. After all, sex was always a hush-hush issue around our house. My mom even taught me about the birds and the bees in the confines of her walk-in closet. My fiancé was surprised, having come from a family where his parents were completely open about physical intimacy. His parents were more than happy to answer any questions their children had, and in the open air! It was a huge relief for me to tell them of my concerns. His mom explained some things to me that really helped. I appreciated their attitude that sex was an exciting and special part of married life.

It is our hope that parents will share a balanced perspective about sexual intimacy with their children, with youth they teach and counsel, and with other adults who may still be struggling to understand the rightful place it has in marriage. But it must be a balanced approach, emphasizing that sex is a holy stewardship reserved exclusively for married couples or young people may feel compelled to experiment with the sacred power of procreation inappropriately. At the same time, it must also clearly inform them of the uplifting and unifying purposes that sexual relations play in marriage. Discussing marital intimacy in a manner that properly educates and prepares, but does not generate inappropriate interests or feelings, is a delicate tight-wire act, but it is possible. And it is required of all parents. The Church counsels:

> The Lord placed upon parents the responsibility to teach their children to understand the proper use of procreative powers. This responsibility cannot be given to another. These powers are to be used only within the sanctity of lawful marriage relationships. As a parent, you can best help your children to see their procreative powers in a pure, chaste, and divine perspective, rather than in the strictly physical view of the world.
>
> You can best teach your children that intimacy between husband and wife must be guided by righteous attitudes toward each other. The most sacred intimacy must be shared in a relationship characterized by genuine love. If we truly love others and desire their eternal joy—if we are our brother's keeper—our intimate relations as husband and wife will uplift rather than degrade. (*A Parent's Guide,* 9.)

When guided by the Spirit, discussions of sexual topics between a parent and child will be among the most rewarding they ever have. The children so instructed will be forever thankful for the counsel they received from wise parents who taught them in a loving and comfortable home setting. It will help them approach intimacy in marriage with realistic expectations, less fear, and an understanding of what it takes to make sexual intimacy a fulfilling part of marriage. This will be the best education a young man or woman can have in preparing for the physical closeness that exists between husband and wife in the holy union of marriage.

Appendix

Prescription Medications That Cause Sexual Dysfunction

(Adapted from Charlton, 37–41, and Maurice, 341–45)

> *Key to potential effects:*
> 1 = Decreased sexual desire
> 2 = Erectile Dysfunction
> 3 = Orgasm impaired, delayed, or absent

Drug	*Potential Effect*
Acetazolamide (Diamox)	1
Alprazolam (Xanax)	3
Amiloride (Midamor)	1, 2
Amoxapine (Asendin)	1, 2, 3
Atenolol (Tenormin)	2
Barbiturates (Phenobarbital)	1, 2
Buproprion (Wellbutrin)	1
Buspirone (BuSpar)	1, 2
Carbamazepine (Tegretol)	2
Chlorpromazine (Thorazine)	1, 2, 3
Chlorthalidone (Hygroton)	1, 2
Cimetidine (Tagamet)	1, 2, 3
Clofibrate (Atromid-S)	1, 2
Clomipramine (Anafranil)	1, 2, 3

Drug	_Potential Effect_
Clonidine (Catapres)	1, 2, 3
Danazol (Danocrine)	1
Dichlorphenamide (Daranide)	2
Digoxin (Lanoxin)	1, 2
Diopyramide (Norpace)	2
Enalapril (Vasotec)	2
Estrogen (birth control pills)	1
Famotidine (Pepcid)	2
Fluoxetine (Prozac)	1, 2
Fluphenazine (Prolixin)	1, 2, 3
Guanabenz (Wytensin)	2
Guanadrel (Hylorel)	1, 2, 3
Guanethidine (Ismelin)	1, 2, 3
Hydrochlorthiazide	2
Imipramine (Tofranil)	1, 2, 3
Indapamide (Lozol)	2
Ketoconazole (Nizoral)	1, 2
Labetolol (Normodyne, Trandate)	2, 3
Lisinopril (Prinivil, Zestril)	1, 2
Lithium (Eskalith)	1, 2
Methadone (Dolophine)	1, 2, 3
Methazolamide (Neptazane)	2
Methyldopa (Aldomet)	1, 2, 3
Metyrosine (Demser)	2, 3
Niacin (Nicolar, Nicor, Nicobid)	1
Nifedipine (Procardia, Adalat)	2
Paroxitine (Paxil)	1, 3
Perphenazine (Trilafon)	3
Phenelzine (Nardil)	2, 3
Phenoxybenzamine (Dibenzyline)	3
Phenytoin (Dilantin)	1, 2
Pimozide (Orap)	2
Prazosin (Minipress)	2
Primidone (Mysoline)	2
Progesterone	1
Propranolol (Inderal)	1, 2

Drug	Potential Effect
Reserpine	1, 2, 3
Sertraline (Zoloft)	1, 3
Spironolactone (Aldactone)	1, 2
Sulpiride (Supril, Sulpitil)	2
Thiabendazole (Mintezol)	2
Thiazide diuretics	2
Thioridazine (Mellaril)	2, 3
Tranylcypromine (Parnate)	2, 3
Venlafaxine (Effexor)	2, 3

Selected Bibliography

ACOG Technical Bulletin, No. 211, September 1995.

Baker, Fred. "Stewardship," *Religion 234 Manual,* Brigham Young University, 303.

Ballard, Melvin J. "The Three Degrees of Glory," (Ogden Tabernacle, 22 September 1922: Deseret Book, pamphlet).

Benson, Ezra Taft. "A Message to the Rising Generation," *Ensign,* November 1977, 30–32.

———. "To The Young Women of the Church," *Ensign,* November 1986, 81–85.

———. "The Law of Chastity," *BYU 1987–1988 Devotional and Fireside Speeches,* Brigham Young University, 49–54.

———. *The Teachings of Ezra Taft Benson* (Salt Lake City: Bookcraft, 1988).

———. "Beware of Pride," *Ensign,* May 1989, 4–6.

Broderick, Carlfred. *Couples* (Simon & Schuster, Inc. New York, 1979).

Brown, Hugh B. *You and Your Marriage* (Salt Lake City: Bookcraft, 1960).

Charlton, Randolph S. ed. *Treating Sexual Disorders* (San Francisco: Jossey-Bass Publishers, 1997).

The Church of Jesus Christ of Latter-day Saints. *A Parent's Guide,* 1985.

Clark, James R. comp. *Messages of the First Presidency,* vol. 4 (Salt Lake City: Bookcraft, 1970).

Faust, James E. "Acting for Ourselves and Not Being Acted Upon," *Ensign,* November 1995, 45–47.

———. "The Grand Key-Words for the Relief Society," *Ensign,* November 1996, 94.

Gottman, John. *Why Marriages Succeed or Fail* (New York: Simon and Schuster, 1994).

Haight, David B. "Marriage and Divorce," *Ensign,* May 1984, 12–14.

Hales, Robert D. "The Eternal Family," *Ensign,* November 1996, 64–67.

Hammond, D. Corydon and Robert F. Stahmann. "Sex Therapy with LDS Couples," *AMCAP Journal,* January 1982, 14.

Hinckley, Gordon B. "Live Up to Your Inheritance," *Ensign,* November 1983, 81–84.

———. "If I Were You, What Would I Do?" *BYU 1983–1984 Fireside and Devotional Speeches,* Brigham Young University, 8–11.

———. "Live the Gospel," *Ensign,* November, 1984, 85–86.

———. "Rise to the Stature of the Divine within You," *Ensign,* November 1989, 97.

———. "Keeping the Temple Holy," *Ensign,* May 1990, 49–52.

———. "What God Hath Joined Together," *Ensign,* May 1991, 71–74.

———. "Message of Inspiration from the Prophet," *Church News,* 30 September 1995, 2.

———. "The Family: A Proclamation to the World," *Ensign,* November 1995, 102.

———. "Speaking Today: A Conversation with Single Adults," *Ensign,* March 1997, 58–63.

———. "Jordan Utah South Regional Conference," *Church News,* 4 October 1997:2.

———. "Walking in the Light of the Lord," *Ensign,* November 1998, 97–100.

Holland, Jeffrey R. "Of Souls, Symbols, and Sacraments," *BYU 1987–88 Devotional and Fireside Speeches,* Brigham Young University, 73–85.

———. "Personal Purity," *Ensign,* November 1998, 75–78.

Huffman, J. W. "The Effect of Gynecologic Surgery on Sexual Reactions," *American Journal of Obstetrics and Gynecology,* 59:915, 1950.

Hunter, Howard W. "Being a Righteous Husband and Father," *Ensign,* November 1994, 49–51.

Kaplan, Helen Singer. *The New Sex Therapy* (New York: Brunner/Mazel, 1974).

———. *Disorders of Sexual Desire* (New York: Simon and Schuster, 1979).

Kimball, Spencer W. "Home Training—the Cure for Evil," *Improvement Era,* June 1965, 514-16.

———. "Guidelines to Carry Forth the Work of God in Cleanliness," *Ensign,* May 1974, 4–8.

————. *The Teachings of Spencer W. Kimball*, Edward L. Kimball, ed. (Salt Lake City: Bookcraft, 1982).

Kolodny, Robert C. et al. *Textbook of Sexual Medicine* (Boston: Little, Brown, and Co., 1979).

Lamb, Stephen E. *Sexual Purity* (Bountiful: Horizon, 1996).

Laumann, Edward O. et al. "Sexual Dysfunction in the United States," *Journal of the American Medical Association*, 10 February 1999 (vol. 281, no. 6) 537.

Lee, Harold B. *The Teachings of Harold B. Lee*, Clyde J. Williams, ed. (Salt Lake City: Bookcraft, 1996).

Leman, Kevin. *Sex Begins in the Kitchen: Because Love Is an All-Day Affair* (Grand Rapids: Fleming H. Revell Company, 1999).

Lundwall, N. B., comp. *Discourses on the Holy Ghost* (Salt Lake City: Bookcraft, 1959).

Masters, William H. and Virginia Johnson. *Human Sexual Inadequacy* (Boston: Little, Brown, and Co., 1970).

Maurice, William L. *Sexual Medicine in Primary Care* (St. Louis: Mosby, 1999).

Maxwell, Neal A. "The Great Plan of the Eternal God," *Ensign*, May, 1984, 21–23.

McConkie, Bruce R. "The Eternal Family Concept," *BYU Second Annual Priesthood Genealogical Research Seminar*, 23 June 1967, unpublished.

————. "Celestial Marriage." *BYU 1977 Devotional Speeches of the Year*, Brigham Young University, 170–74.

————. "The Ten Blessings of the Priesthood," *Ensign*, November 1977, 33–35.

McKay, David O. "Something Higher than Self," *Improvement Era*, June 1958, 406–409.

Nakhnikian, Elise. "Sex Therapy Is Alive and Well," *Self*, September, 1991, 185.

Oaks, Dallin H. "The Great Plan of Happiness," *Ensign*, November 1993, 72–75.

————. "Apostasy and Restoration," *Ensign*, May 1995, 84–87.

Packer, Boyd K. "Church Relief Society Conference," *Salt Lake Tribune*, 2 October 1971, sec. B1.

————. "Why Stay Morally Clean," *Ensign*, July 1972, 111–113.

————. "Marriage," *Ensign*, May 1981, 13–15.

————. "The Fountain of Life," BYU 18-Stake Fireside Address, 29 March 1992, unpublished.

————. "Our Moral Environment," *Ensign*, May 1992, 66–68.

————. "The Shield of Faith," *Ensign*, May 1995, 7–9.

————. "Washed Clean," *Ensign*, May 1997, 9–11.

————. "The Relief Society," *Ensign*, May 1998, 72–74.

Pratt, Parley P. *Key to the Science of Theology*, 9th edition (Salt Lake City: Deseret Book, 1965).

Richards, Claude. *J. Golden Kimball: The Story of a Unique Personality* (Salt Lake City: Bookcraft, 1966).

Rinehart, John S. and Isaac Schiff. *Human Sexuality: Psychosexual Effects of Disease*, Martin Farber, ed. (New York: MacMillan, 1985).

Robinson, Parker P. *The Writings of Parley Parker Pratt* (Salt Lake City: Deseret News Press, 1952).

Romney, Marion G. "The Way of Life," *Ensign*, May 1976, 79–81.

Rudy, D. R. "Sexual Dysfunction after Hysterectomy," *Contemporary Ob/Gyn*, March 1993, 40.

Rytting, Lori E. "Sterilization," *Encyclopedia of Mormonism*, 4 vols., Daniel H. Ludlow ed. (New York: MacMillan, 1992), 1417.

Scott, Richard G. "Making the Right Choice," *Ensign*, November 1994, 37–39.

————. "To Live the Great Plan of Happiness," *Ensign*, November 1996, 73-75.

Smith, Joseph. *History of The Church of Jesus Christ of Latter-day Saints*, B. H. Roberts, ed. (Salt Lake City: Deseret Book, 1973).

Smith, Joseph F. *Gospel Doctrine* (Salt Lake City: Deseret Book, 1919).

Smith, Joseph Fielding, ed. *Teachings of the Prophet Joseph Smith* (Salt Lake City: Deseret Book, 1972).

Tanner, N. Eldon. "The Blessing of Church Interviews," *Ensign*, November 1978, 40–43.

Taylor, John. *The Government of God* (Liverpool: S. W. Richards, 1852).

————. *The Gospel Kingdom*, 3rd edition, G. Homer Durham, ed. (Salt Lake City: Bookcraft, 1944).

Wernick, Nissim. "Man, the Pinnacle of Creation," *BYU Studies*, 10:1 (Autumn 1969) 31–42.

Widtsoe, John A. *Discourses of Brigham Young* (Salt Lake City: Deseret Book, 1941).

Index